ADIRONDACK HIGH SCHOOL
8181 STATE ROUTE 294
BOONVILLE, NY 13309
A1J

D1528507

The Fight for
LATINO CIVIL RIGHTS

Bárbara C. Cruz

Enslow Publishing
101 W. 23rd Street
Suite 240
New York, NY 10011
USA

Published in 2016 by Enslow Publishing, LLC
101 W. 23rd Street, Suite 240, New York, NY 10011

Cataloging-in-Publication Data
Cruz, Bárbara C.
The fight for Latino civil rights / by Bárbara C. Cruz.
p. cm. — (Our shared history)
Includes bibliographical references and index.
ISBN 978-0-7660-7006-6 (library binding)
1. Hispanic Americans -—Civil rights — History — Juvenile literature. 2. Immigrants -—Civil rights — United
States — History — Juvenile literature. 3. Civil rights movements — United States —History — Juvenile literature.
I. Cruz, Bárbara. II. Title.
E184.S75 C78 2016
323.119468073—d23

Printed in the United States of America

To Our Readers: We have done our best to make sure all Web site addresses in this book were active and
appropriate when we went to press. However, the author and the publisher have no control over and assume
no liability for the material available on those Web sites or any Web sites they may link to. Any comments
or suggestions can be sent by e-mail to customerservice@enslow.com.

Portions of this book originally appeared in the book *Triumphs and Struggles for Latino Civil Rights*.

Photo Credits: © 2015 Florida State Hispanic Chamber of Commerce, p. 140; © AP Images, pp. 8, 34, 44, 57,
65, 76, 80, 82, 84, 87, 89, 96, 100, 115; Arthur Schatz/The LIFE Images Collection/Getty Images, p. 4; CBS Photo
Archive/Getty Images, p. 131; Charles Trainor Jr./Miami Herald Staff, p. 76; David Livingston/Getty Images
Entertainment/Getty Images, p. 109; David McNew/Getty Images News/Getty Images, p. 138; Education Images/
UIG via Getty Images, p. 21; Ethan Miller/Getty Images Entertainment/Getty Images, p. 135; Ethan Miller/
Getty Images Entertainment/Getty Images for Keep Memory Alive, p. 129; Focus on Sport/Getty Images, p.
124; Fotosearch/Archive Photos/Getty Images, p. 95; George Rose/Hulton Archive/Getty Images, p. 111; ilolab/
Shutterstock.com (textured background throughout book); James Garrett/NY Daily News Archive via Getty
Images, p. 39; JFK Library/National Park Service/US Department of the Interior, p. 41; Joel Page/Portland
Press Herald via Getty Images, p. 117; John Moore/Getty Images News/Getty Images, p. 79; Jonathan Barrera
Mikulich, Latino Branding Power, p. 104; Klaus Vedfelt/Taxi/Getty Images, p. 67; Lawrence Lucier/Getty Images
Entertainment/ Getty Images, p. 114; LCDM Universal History Archive/Universal Images Group/Getty Images,
p. 21; Library of Congress, Prints and Photographs Division (chapter head photos throughout book), pp.10,
19; Library of Congress, Prints & Photographs Division, Visual Materials from the NAACP Records [LC-
USZ62-75515], p. 33; "MAPPING THE LATINO POPULATION, BY
STATE, COUNTY AND CITY" Pew Research Center, Washington, DC (August, 2013) http://www.pewhispanic.
org/2013/08/29/mapping-the-latino-population-by-state-county-and-city/; Mark Crosse/Fresno Bee/MCT via
Getty Images, p. 113; Megan Q. Daniels/ First Light/Getty Images, p. 103; NASA/Hulton Archive/Liaison/Getty
Images, p. 121; © Niday Picture Library/Alamy, p. 93; © North Wind Picture Archives, p. 23; Pascal Le Segretain/
Getty Images Entertainment/Getty Images, p. 136; PAUL BUCK/AFP/Getty Images, p. 126; PAUL ELLIS/AFP/
Getty Images, p. 128; Paul Marotta/Getty Images Entertainment/Getty Images, p. 107; Photo courtesy of Ivonne
Blank, p. 29; Photo courtesy of NASA, p. 119; Rusinow/United States Department of Agriculture/Wikimedia
Commons/SchoolLunch.jpg/public domain, p. 53; Scanlan/United States Congress/Wikimedia Commons/Ileana
Ros-Lehtinen Congressional Portrait.jpg/public domain, p. 46; The National Association of Latino Elected and
Appointed Officials NALEO, p. 42; ullstein bild/ullstein bild via Getty Images, p. 50; US Army Center of Military
History, p. 24; US Army photo by Spc. Wilma Orozco Fanfan, 113th Mobile Public Affairs Detachment, 101st
Troop Command, Puerto Rico Army National Guard, p. 122; US Census Bureau, p. 15; US Census Bureau/
Wikimedia Commons/US Census 1990 hispanic.jpg/public domain, p. 74; US Department of Defense/Wikimedia
Commons/Felix-longoria-photo-01.jpg/public domain, p. 27; "U.S. Hispanic Country of Origin Counts for
Nation, Top 30 Metropolitan Areas" Pew Research Center, Washington, DC (May, 2011)http://www.pewhispanic.
org/2011/05/26/us-hispanic-country-of-origin-counts-for-nation-top-30-metropolitan-areas/; Wehwalt/
University of California, Bancroft Library/Wikimedia Commons/Bakke protest 1.jpg/public domain, p. 61.

Cover Credits: David McNew/Getty Images News/Getty Images (immigrant rights activists); ilolab/Shutterstock.
com (textured background).

CONTENTS

César Chávez was a labor leader and activist who fought for the rights of Latino American workers.

The Struggle for Rights

"...Across California, across the entire nation, wherever there are injustices against men and women and children who work in the fields—there you will see our flags...Our movement is spreading like flames across a dry plain." [1]

—César Chávez

The pilgrims made their way on their long journey. Despite their pain and fatigue, they tried to stay focused on their goal: to improve conditions for migrant farm workers. The march through California had been organized by César Chávez, the National Farm Workers Association (NFWA), and the Agricultural Workers Organizing Committee (AWOC). In the winter of 1966 they had planned the 340-mile march from Delano, where Chávez lived, to Sacramento, the capital of California. Chávez had planned the march to begin on March 17 and end on Easter Sunday. Because it would be during the Lenten season, Chávez called it a *peregrinación*, or pilgrimage. A pilgrimage is a long journey usually taken for a moral or spiritual purpose. Lent refers to the forty-day period before Easter in Christianity. It is a holy time marked by fasting and personal sacrifice.

Chávez knew firsthand how hard life could be as a migrant farm worker. His own family had lost their farm in Arizona during the Great Depression, and they had been forced to look for work as migrant farmers. Now, in 1966, most farm workers lived in the cramped quarters of labor camps, often ten or more people in a trailer home. Usually their housing had no bathrooms, no electricity, and no running water.

In 1965 Chávez had joined a strike and boycott of table grapes initiated by the Filipino grape workers who were members of the AWOC. A year later, the farm owners still had not made enough changes to improve the workers' dismal conditions. Chávez knew something dramatic needed to be done to call attention to the farm workers' struggle.

After just the first day of the march in 1966, painful blisters covered the marchers' feet. One marcher said, "Some people had bloody feet. Some would keep on walking and you'd see blood coming out of their shoes."[2] One of Chávez's legs swelled, and he developed a high fever. Despite the severe pain and the fever, Chávez refused medication and continued on the march, using a cane to help him walk.

Each night when the marchers stopped, they held a meeting to rally support and to educate the public. Hundreds of families hosted the marchers in each

César Chávez

César Chávez was born on March 31, 1927, near Yuma, Arizona. Although the Chávez family was far from rich, they led a comfortable life with everyone in the family helping in the family business—a combination grocery store, garage, and pool hall.

Then in 1929 the Great Depression changed the family's life forever. Just like millions of other Americans who lost their jobs and homes, the Chávez family was forced to sell their business. Like thousands of others, the family left their home and moved to California in search of jobs.

César's family became migrant farm workers. As his parents followed the harvest of different fruits and vegetables, César and his siblings helped pick crops and went to school when they could. César and his family sometimes lived in migrant worker camps. Other times, they had no choice but to camp out under bridges and in shacks made out of cardboard and tar paper.

These painful memories would serve Chávez well. Knowing from firsthand experience how hard life could be as a farm laborer, Chávez went on to create the UFW shortly after his famous march in 1966. Today the UFW continues its work to protect and represent farm workers throughout the United States.

César Chávez walks in the 1966 march that he organized in order to get the word out about the farm workers' strike.

town, offering them a meal, a shower, and a bed to rest in preparation for the next day's walk.

As the procession worked its way through the small towns, hundreds of people greeted the marchers and sometimes joined them, helping them carry their flags to the next town. The march eventually took twenty-five grueling days.

When the march ended on Easter Sunday as planned, about ten thousand people joined Chávez and the marchers on the steps of the capitol. Dr. Martin Luther King Jr. sent Chávez a telegram. In it, Dr. King sent his best wishes to Chávez and the United Farm Workers (UFW): "Our separate struggles are really one—a struggle for freedom, for dignity, and for humanity . . . We are together with you in spirit and in determination that our dreams for a better tomorrow will be realized."[3] Like African Americans, Hispanic Americans have had to work hard to ensure that their rights are respected and protected.

Chávez and his associates later established the UFW. They worked tirelessly to improve the lives of agricultural workers, bringing awareness of their terrible conditions to the American public. They started a boycott of table grapes, an industry that did not treat workers well. Those Americans who supported the UFW responded by not buying table grapes. By 1969 almost three quarters of the California grape growers were out of business. By the spring of 1970, an agreement between the remaining growers and the union was finally signed. No one could believe that ordinary citizens had triumphed over the rich

César Chávez's United Farm Workers (UFW) did not end their fight for rights in the 1960s. This 1978 UFW poster promotes a boycott of lettuce and grapes.

and powerful growers. Chávez was especially pleased when, in 1975, California passed the Agricultural Labor Relations Act, which recognized the rights of farm workers to organize and bargain collectively.

Chávez's determined struggle for justice is but one story among many in the history of Latinos in the United States. And the struggle for justice and equality continues today.

Latino Americans

 Latinos go by different names. Some prefer to simply use the term *Hispanic* or *Latino*. Many others refer to the specific country of origin, for example, Colombian American, Cuban American, or Mexican American. Many Mexican Americans prefer the term *Chicano*, an identification that has political implications and reflects ethnic pride. Some Puerto Ricans called themselves *Boriqua* or even *Nuyorican* if they are from New York. Some Latinos prefer to use the term "Latin@s," which includes Latinas and Latinos (females and males) as a whole group.[1]

There are at least two ways to identify Latinos. There are those whose ancestors have been in the United States for generations but still retain the culture and/or language of their native country. There are also recent immigrants from Spanish-speaking countries who are considered Latino. The US Census Bureau defines a Hispanic or Latino citizen as "a

I am Joaquín—
Yo Soy Joaquín

Rodolfo "Corky" Gonzales published his poem *Yo Soy Joaquín* (*I Am Joaquín*) in 1967. In it, Gonzales shared his new cosmological idea of the "Chicano," a person who is neither Indian nor European, neither Mexican nor American, but a mixture of many identities. It encouraged Chicano youths to find pride in their culture and history.

Juan Felipe Herrera, a professor at the University of California at Riverside, remembered that when the poem was published, it caused a sensation throughout the Latino community. Herrera says, "Here, finally, was our collective song, and it arrived like thunder crashing down from the heavens. Every little barrio newspaper from Albuquerque to Berkeley published it. People slapped mimeographed copies up on walls and telephone poles."[2]

person of Cuban, Mexican, Puerto Rican, South or Central American, or other Spanish culture or origin regardless of race."[3] As of 2012, there were 54 million Latinos, the largest ethnic minority in the United States.[4]

Latinos are not one culture or one nationality. They are people whose families have origins in South America, Central America, Mexico, or the Spanish-speaking Caribbean. Today, about 17 percent of the US population is made up of Latinos.[5] The states with the largest concentrations of Latinos are California, Colorado, Arizona, New Mexico, Texas, Florida, Illinois, New York, and New Jersey.

The terms *Hispanic* and *Latino* are used more or less interchangeably in the United States. However, for some people the use of the terms is controversial. The federal government commonly uses Hispanic, but many argue that the term tends to stress European (Spanish) roots. Some people favor Latino because it puts more emphasis on Latin-American origins.

Many Latinos emphasize their *mestizaje*, that is, their "mixed" heritage of European, native, African, and Asian peoples. According to the 2010 US Census, over eighteen million Hispanics (36.7%) indicated "some other race" besides White, Black, or African American.[6] Like many people of mixed ancestry, they resent having to select one group over another to identify themselves. For example, a person with one Chinese parent and one Latino parent might call herself "China-Latina."

Afro-Latinos make up at least 3 percent of Latinos in the United States.[8] However, this figure is probably much higher. Because "race" is understood differently throughout Latin America, Latinos' self-identification is likely to differ also. Of the estimated twelve million African slaves inhumanely brought to the New World, 91 percent were taken to Latin America and the Caribbean.[11] This diaspora, or scattering of people

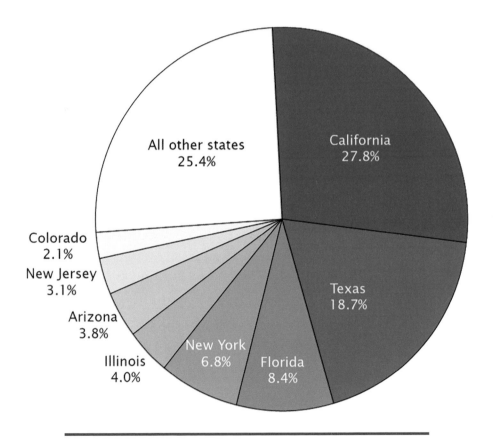

This graph shows the percentage of Latinos in the United States broken down by state as of 2010.[7]

Latinos by the Numbers[9]

In 2011 Latinos become the largest (17%) minority ethnic group in the United States.

- By the year 2060, Latinos will constitute 31% of the US population.
- Only Mexico has a larger Hispanic population than the United States.
- More than one-third of Hispanic Americans were born in another country.
- More than 50% of the nation's Latinos live in California, Florida, and Texas.
- 13% of US residents five years and older speak Spanish at home. More than half of these Spanish speakers also speak English "very well."

The Distribution of the Nation's Hispanic Population, 2011
Hispanic population share by county

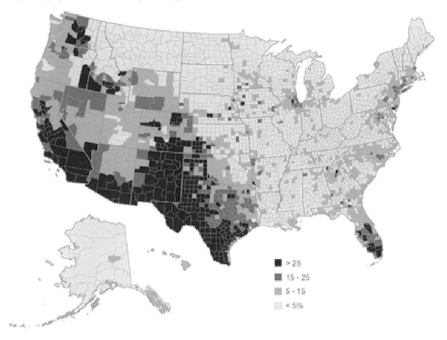

> ■ > 25
> ■ 15 - 25
> ▨ 5 - 15
> □ < 5%

Source: U.S. Census Bureau county population datasets

PEW RESEARCH CENTER

This map shows that the counties with the highest Hispanic populations are mostly in the southwestern United States.[10]

far away from their ancestral lands, resulted in rich cultural traditions and contributions.

While they seem to be one of the latest immigrant groups to enter the United States, Latinos have been a vital force in the nation's history since before the English settled in Jamestown, Virginia, in 1607.

Celia Cruz

One of the most beloved salsa singers of all time, Celia Cruz was born in Havana, Cuba, on October 21, 1925. An Afro-Cuban, Celia grew up in a diverse neighborhood with a strong music tradition. She entered singing contests and impressed judges and audiences with her powerful voice.

Celia's father encouraged her to become a teacher so she enrolled at the National Teachers' College. But Celia's heart was in music. To please her father and stay in school, Celia switched to Havana's National Conservatory of Music. But soon one of Celia's professors heard her sing and persuaded her to leave her studies and pursue a professional singing career.

One of the most famous orchestras in Cuba was the Sonora Matancera. In 1950, they needed a new lead singer. At first, it was uncertain if Cruz could successfully replace the popular previous singer. But audiences immediately were won over by the energetic and elegant Cruz. Soon she and the band began touring throughout Latin America and the United States.

In 1959 a Communist takeover led by Fidel Castro and Ernesto "Ché" Guevara led to a new form of government. While the band was performing in Mexico in 1960, Cruz and others decided to defect. Cruz and the Sonora Matancera settled in New York. In retaliation, the Cuban government banned them from returning to the island.

Over the next forty years Cruz's fan base grew. With her colorful costumes, charming personality, and dynamic singing style, she sold out concerts, won several Grammy Awards, and earned a star on Hollywood's Walk of Fame. In 1994 Cruz received the National Medal of the Arts from President Bill Clinton.

Celia Cruz died July 16, 2003, at the age of 77.

Celia Cruz was a Cuban-born American who was best known for her dynamic salsa performances.

History of Latinos in the United States

"Hispanics are fully as American as every other person because they share their faith in the enduring truth of the nature of equal rights, freedom, respect, and opportunity."[1]

—Mel Martinez, US Senator and former Pedro Pan child

Many historians point out that the first Thanksgiving was actually held by Spanish colonists in St. Augustine, Florida. Fifty-five years before the English Pilgrims landed at Plymouth Rock, the St. Augustine settlers held a religious service and gathered for a meal with the native people. The oldest city on the US mainland, St. Augustine was established by Spanish soldiers in 1565.

When Christopher Columbus sailed to the Americas in 1492, he sailed under the Spanish flag for King Ferdinand and Queen Isabella. Many other Spanish explorers, such as Juan Ponce de León, were sent in the years that followed to find gold, silver, and other riches.

In addition to the riches they were seeking, the Spanish also sent Catholic priests to protect the explorers and to spread the word of Christianity. These friars, also called missionaries, often converted the native people to Catholicism. Some of these priests established missions—religious outposts that often became the heart of new communities. As land was claimed, the Spanish empire grew in the Americas so that eventually it included much of the present-day United States, Mexico, and most of Central and South America.

One of the most well-known missionaries was Father Junípero Serra, a Franciscan priest. In 1769 he founded a mission in California in the San Diego area. Eventually, twenty-one missions were established throughout what is now the state of California, from San Francisco in the north to San Diego in the south. The Spanish founded other missions in the Southwest including New Mexico, Arizona, and Texas.

As the colonists sought independence from Great Britain, the Hispanic presence continued to grow. As the American patriots rebelled against English rule, many Hispanics outside the British colo-

Father Junípero Serra

nies aligned themselves with the revolutionaries. Bernardo de Gálvez, governor of Louisiana, helped George Washington and his men during the American Revolution. He aided the Americans in their fight against the British by allowing badly needed supplies to be shipped up the Mississippi River to patriot forces in the north. Later Gálvez commanded troops in battle against the British. In Cuba, the "Havana Ladies" donated their jewelry and diamonds to finance the battle of Yorktown.[2] *Las Damas de la Havana* were able to raise over one million pounds sterling.

Once the new nation was established, people started moving west as the US government gave more and more incentives for settling. As people moved into areas that had been originally inhabited by American Indians and Spanish-speaking people, clashes inevitably ensued.

In 1836 Texas, still a possession of Mexico, declared itself independent. The disagreement marked the beginning of the Mexican-American War. The war ended with the signing of the Treaty of Guadalupe Hidalgo in 1848. Through this agreement, the United States gained not only Texas but also New Mexico, California, and parts of several other states. As a result, Mexico lost half its national territory.

Instantaneously, about seventy-eight thousand residents of these lands became US citizens. Just a few years later, in 1853 Mexico sold land to the United States by means of the Gadsden Purchase. This treaty covered thirty thousand square miles of land that included parts of Arizona and New Mexico, south of

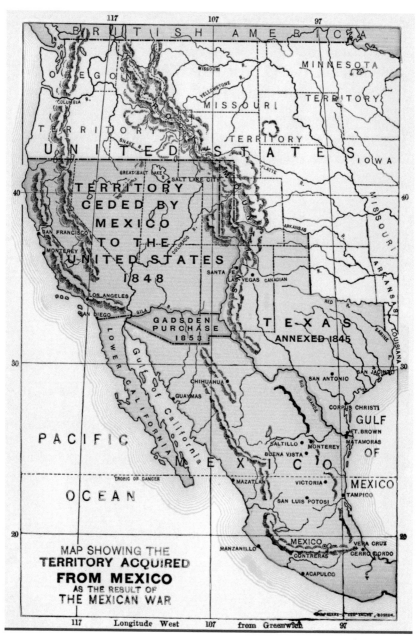

As a result of the Mexican-American War, the United States gained a large amount of land, including Texas, Utah, Nevada, and California.

the Gila River. All of this land amounted to what some Mexican Americans later called "The Lost Land."

During the US Civil War, Hispanics also left their mark on American history. About ten thousand Hispanics fought in the conflict, serving for both the Confederacy and the Union. Two Hispanic Union Navy servicemen, Philip Bazaar and John Ortega, won the Congressional Medal of Honor. Cuban-American Loreta Janeta Velázquez disguised herself as a man to fight for the Confederacy. Only after she was injured in battle was her identity revealed. David G. Farragut, son of Spanish immigrant Jorge Farragut, was the Navy's first four-star admiral. In the Civil War's Battle of New Orleans, he gave his famous order, "Damn the torpedoes! Full steam ahead!"

American troops enter San Juan, Puerto Rico, during the 1898 Spanish-American War.

As the United States was battling its own bloody civil war, in the Caribbean, Cuba and Puerto Rico began fighting for their independence from Spain. After the USS *Maine* blew up in Havana Harbor in 1898, the United States entered the war against Spain. After five months of fighting, the Spanish-American War was brought to a close in 1898. In a treaty signed between Spain and the United States, Cuba was freed from Spanish control. Spain also gave the territories of Puerto Rico, Guam, and the Philippines to the United States. Cuba and the Philippines eventually became independent nations, but Puerto Rico and Guam became "possessions" of the United States.

The US Congress passed the Platt Amendment in 1902. Under this law the United States could intervene in Cuban matters at any time. Presumably, this was to maintain Cuba's independence and stability. But critics argued that Cuba was free in name only and that the United States *really* controlled the island nation.

In 1917 the Jones Act granted all Puerto Ricans US citizenship. The act did not allow Puerto Ricans to vote in national elections but it did make them eligible for the military draft. While many welcomed the new status, many native Puerto Ricans protested the act, saying that it was just a ploy to increase the pool of eligible draftees for World War I. Many also believed that it would keep Puerto Rico from ever becoming independent.

Right after World War I, South Americans started coming to the United States in large numbers. Many of the new immigrants settled in the Jackson Heights neighborhood of New York City. Even today, it is the largest South American community in the United States. People from places such as Ecuador, Peru, and Colombia have created a vibrant community there.

In 1929, when the stock market crashed and heralded the beginning of the Great Depression, Latinos were especially hard hit. As people lost their jobs and homes, the government began to repatriate, or return, as many immigrants as possible to their homeland to free up resources. In particular, about one million Mexican immigrants left the United States and returned to Mexico.

The 1930s saw a steady influx of Puerto Ricans to New York City. Many of them settled into a neighborhood that eventually was called Spanish Harlem or, simply, *El Barrio* (the neighborhood). After World War II, the flow from Puerto Rico to the United States (especially New York City) increased greatly. Today there are more Puerto Ricans living in New York than in San Juan, the capital of Puerto Rico.

In 1959 Fidel Castro, Ernesto "Ché" Guevara, and their associates overthrew the government of Fulgencio Batista in Cuba. When Castro officially became the prime minister, he suspended the Constitution and assumed total power. Castro and his government took over private businesses and made them public property. Opponents to his government were imprisoned or executed. The United States' initial fear that Castro would turn the country toward communism was realized when Cuba aligned itself with the Soviet Union.

Private Félix Longoria

Despite their service, Latinos were not always treated equally in the military. One case that made this unequal treatment painfully real was the case of Private Félix Longoria. In 1948, the body of Private Longoria, who was a Mexican American, was recovered from the Philippines. Private Longoria had been killed on a mission and his remains were sent home for burial with honors.

In Longoria's hometown of Three Rivers, Texas, the cemetery was separated into two sections: one for Mexicans and one for Anglos (white, non-Hispanic Americans). Barbed wire separated the two. The director of the town's only funeral home refused to allow the Longoria family to use the chapel.

With the help of Dr. Héctor García, a war veteran who had created an organization to provide

Private Félix Longoria

Latino veterans with adequate health care, Longoria's widow contacted the press and Texas congressmen to seek their support. Lyndon B. Johnson, then a senator, arranged for a burial at Arlington National Cemetery. Finally, on February 16, 1949, the Longoria family, accompanied by Senator Johnson, was able to bury Private Longoria with full military honors. While the delay of the burial was a tragic reminder of the discrimination that existed in the country, it was also encouraging that the US government was paying attention to Hispanics' struggle for civil rights.[3]

Operación Pedro Pan
December 26, 1960–October 23, 1962

Soon after Fidel Castro's revolution in Cuba, rumors spread throughout the island that the new socialist government would take children away from their parents and send them to schools and work camps in the Soviet Union.

With the help of the Catholic Church, frightened families began sending their children alone to Miami in a program that became known as Operación Pedro Pan (Operation Peter Pan). Supported by the US government, more than fourteen thousand Cuban children arrived in the United States. About half went to live with family members already in the United States. The rest were placed with host American families and orphanages in thirty states that volunteered to take in the children.[4]

While most families assumed they would soon be reunited, the Cuban Missile Crisis of 1962 disrupted unification efforts and some of the children remained separated from their families for years.

Despite the challenges faced by the Pedro Pan children, they have enjoyed great success in their new homeland, becoming professionals such as teachers, doctors, and journalists.[5] Some of the more well-known Pedro Pan children include Willy Chirino, popular salsa musician; US Senator Mel Martinez; and artist Ana Mendieta.

Ivonne Garay (center) poses with two girls at a camp for Pedro Pan children in Florida City in 1962.

Thousands of Cubans fled the island and settled in the United States, primarily in Miami, Florida, in an area that became known as "Little Havana." Many of the Cuban refugees planned to return home once the revolution subsided. However, that did not occur. With the realization that they would never be able to return to their homeland, they began making the United States their permanent home.

Cuban immigrants slowly trickled into the United States in the years that followed the Cuban Revolution. But in 1980, a large group of about 125,000 refugees arrived from the port of Mariel. Known as *Marielitos*, their arrival at first led to anti-immigrant feelings.

Eventually, the Marielitos found a way to become part of American society.

Dominicans also form a large part of the Latino population in the United States. The tangled history of the Dominican Republic and the United States goes back to at least 1916, when political and economic turmoil prompted the United States to occupy the island. With a military government in place, the occupation ended in 1924, when a new government was democratically elected.

The peace was short lived, however. In 1930, military leader Rafael L. Trujillo took over the government. While Trujillo promoted some economic development, he was known for brutally repressing human rights. He stayed in power until 1961, when he was assassinated.

Trujillo's assassination led to relaxed immigration laws. In 1965, with the Dominican Republic embattled in civil war, the United States invaded Santo Domingo.

Hoping to influence the victory of a pro-American government, US forces monitored elections that saw the victory of Joaquín Balaguer. Thousands of Dominicans came to the United States, settling in New York City's Washington Heights neighborhood.

The history of Latinos in the United States, in many respects, has only just begun. As the largest ethnic minority group in the United States, Latinos and Latin American immigrants will continue to make their mark for years to come.

Legal and Civil Rights

As World War II raged, a group of sailors and marines were on shore leave in Los Angeles, California. Some of them claimed that a gang of pachucos had attacked them. *Pachucos* were Chicanos (Mexican Americans) who wore "zoot suits." In the 1940s, this popular form of dress was made up of loosely fitting pants with a high waist and narrow cuffs at the ankles. It was topped with a long jacket with wide, padded shoulders and a long key chain. Thick-soled shoes and wide-brimmed, flat "porkpie" hats completed the look. Many people associated this style of dress with gangs and violence, but like teenagers in every era, the pachucos just wanted their own special look and identity.

A group of over two hundred sailors in uniform stormed into a Mexican-American neighborhood in East Los Angeles. The sailors attacked anyone wearing a zoot suit. The servicemen tore off the pachucos' clothing, beat them, and left them in the streets.

The assaults occurred for several more nights. Civilians began participating in the assaults as well. The riots spread to other cities in California, Texas, Chicago, and New York. Chicanos were singled out on the streets, pulled from buses, and dragged from movie theaters to be beaten.[1]

These attacks are known today as the Zoot Suit Riots. The police did not stop the sailors, believing like many in the community that the beatings would halt an alleged "Mexican crime wave." Hundreds of Mexican-American youths were arrested without cause. The police said that the arrests were "preventive."[2] The Mexican ambassador demanded that the attacks cease. The military police finally stopped the assaults on the fifth night when they forbade the servicemen from going to Los Angeles. However, it was an important lesson for Latinos, who realized that they needed to organize politically to protect their civil rights.

Organizing for Change

The oldest Latino organization in the United States is the League of United Latin American Citizens (LULAC). Founded in Texas in 1929, LULAC works for Latinos' rights in education, employment, health, housing, and immigration. In 1954 LULAC took on the state of Texas in the landmark case, *Hernández v. the State of Texas*. Up until that time, no one of Mexican origin had ever been called to jury duty in at least seventy counties in Texas. LULAC attorneys took the case to the Supreme Court. The Supreme Court

The Zoot Suit Riots took place in Los Angeles in 1943. Sailors and Marines clashed with young Latino men for several nights, often attacking with wooden clubs like the ones shown here.

ruled this exclusion unconstitutional, ensuring the right for Mexican Americans to serve on juries.

The Community Services Organization (CSO) was another group that fought for Latino civil rights. Founded in 1947, two of its most visible organizers were Fred Ross and César Chávez. Ross and Chávez used effective organizing methods such as the "house meeting" approach.[3] This strategy meant gathering people at a trusted coworker's house where they felt more comfortable than in a large, public hall. All the people attending would then be asked to host a meeting in their homes so that even more new people could be brought into the movement.

The CSO emphasized voter registration and voter education so that voters could make wise, informed decisions at the polls. By getting more of the workers registered to vote, they would have the power to elect officials and have a voice in government. Chávez was so effective at getting Mexican Americans registered to vote that he was soon assigned the job of helping Mexican immigrants become US citizens. In 1959 Chávez became the CSO's executive director in California.

The Mexican American Political Association (MAPA), founded in 1960 in California, strives to represent Hispanics in the political arena. MAPA works toward the social, economic, and civic betterment of all Spanish-speaking Americans through

CSO members encouraged farm workers to vote in elections. César Chávez, one of the group's leaders, is pictured on the right.

political action. It sponsors community rallies, holds conferences on important issues, and calls for economic boycotts to bring attention to problems faced by Latinos in the United States.

In 1968 the Mexican American Legal Defense and Education Fund (MALDEF) was created. Known as "the legal arm of the Latino community," MALDEF works to foster sound public policies, laws, and programs that protect the rights of Latinos. MALDEF's legal work includes immigration reform, fair voting and citizenship rights, and employment opportunities.

Another organization created during the 1960s was the National Council of La Raza (NCLR). Still very active, this organization focuses on improving opportunities for Latinos by reducing poverty and discrimination. It is a not-for-profit association that is not tied to any political party. NCLR is the largest national Latino civil rights organization in the United States. Its focus on five key areas—assets/investments, civil rights/immigration, education, employment, and health—helps to provide opportunities for individuals and families. NCLR's headquarters is in Washington, DC, but it is active in forty-one states.

In the political arena, the Raza Unida Party (RUP) was created as an alternative to the traditional two-party system in the United States. Founded in Texas in 1970 by José Angel Gutiérrez and Mario Compean, the RUP's original goal was to improve conditions for Latinos throughout Texas. The party soon spread to other states as well. In September 1972, the party held its first national convention. Meeting in

El Paso, Texas, the party's platform included workers' and women's rights, bilingual education, and environmental protection. The party had its share of in-house problems, however, including political disagreements, financial mismanagement, and the arrest of one gubernatorial candidate on drug charges. Eventually, the power and tradition of the two-party system was too strong and the RUP was disbanded in 1981.

Today, there are many active political organizations that assist Latinos. *Mi Familia Vota!* (My Family Votes!) is a voter registration project launched by People for the American Way. The project reaches out to unregistered Latinos eligible to vote. Strategies to reach potential voters include going door-to-door, making presentations in community centers, and even setting up information booths in places like supermarkets, barber shops, and cultural festivals. To date, the *Mi Familia Vota!* project has empowered Latino communities by helping Latinos become US citizens and registering them to vote.

ASPIRA is perhaps the most well-known program among Latino youth because of its ASPIRA Clubs in schools. Led by Dr. Antonia Pantoja, a group of Puerto Rican professionals established ASPIRA in 1961. By focusing on education and leadership development, they hoped to promote self-esteem and cultural pride. Many of these "aspirantes" went on to become leaders in their communities and helped to train another generation.

Latinos United

In addition to formal organizations, Latinos have also organized at the grassroots level. Individuals and groups of citizens have come together at different times to better the lives of Latinos.

Rodolfo "Corky" Gonzales, a Chicano poet, boxer, and political activist is regarded as one of the early founders of the Chicano Movement, which demanded equal rights for Mexican Americans. In 1968 Gonzales convened the first-ever Chicano youth conference. At the gathering, he unveiled his *Plan Espiritual de Aztlán*. This manifesto (a public declaration of beliefs and policies) demanded that Chicanos be allowed to determine their own political status. Gonzales led demonstrations, boycotts, and student walkouts protesting police brutality, inferior housing, and what he called "the educational neglect of Mexican Americans."[4]

During the civil rights movement, students were very involved in politics. One group of Chicano students, the Brown Berets, organized themselves to bring attention to the discrimination that Latinos faced. Many people think of them as the Latino version of the African-American Black Panthers. Originally called the Young Chicanos for Community Action, these high school students decided to wear brown berets as a symbol of unity and pride in being brown, rather than black or white. Soon they became known as the "Brown Berets." The Brown Berets were committed to fighting police harassment, unfair educational practices, a lack of political representation, and the Vietnam War. They became known for leading walkouts, where high school and college students were encouraged to walk out of their classrooms to protest injustice. The group eventually disbanded in 1972.

The Young Lords was another student activist group similar to the Black Panthers. Active in the 1950s and 1960s in Chicago and New York, these young Puerto Rican Americans organized protests and demonstrations to bring public attention to a number of problems. They worked tirelessly on issues such as health care, women's rights, and prisoners' rights. They created a "13-Point Program" that called for things such as liberation for Puerto Rico, equality for women, and an end to racism.[5] The Young Lords were able to set up free breakfasts for schoolchildren, community health tests, clothing drives, and many community events that showed their pride in Puerto Rican culture and history. The group was controversial, however, because it advocated armed self-defense and a socialist society.

One of the issues that the Young Lords focused on was education. The low college acceptance rates for Puerto Ricans and African Americans led to the 1969 sit-in at the south campus of the City University of New York. Students locked themselves in several buildings and forced the school to close down. They asked for an open admissions policy, Black and Puerto Rican studies programs, and Spanish classes for all education majors.

The Young Lords was an activist group made up of Puerto Rican students protesting the plight of Puerto Ricans and all Latinos.

Community members responded by bringing food and blankets to the protesters. There were skirmishes with the police, and after dozens of student activists were arrested, the takeover finally ended. The Young Lords were instrumental in establishing a more open college admissions policy, the creation of Puerto Rican studies programs, and the establishment of several student organizations.

While many of these student groups no longer exist, one student group, MEChA, is still active on college campuses throughout the United States. MEChA (*Movimiento Estudiantil Chican@ de Aztlán;* in English, Chicano Student Movement of Aztlán) seeks to promote awareness of Chicano history through education and political action. Founded in 1969, the group's motto quickly became *La Unión Hace La Fuerza* (Unity Creates Strength). MEChA was instrumental in the creation of Chicano studies programs and departments.

The Civil Rights Act

Although many people associate the Civil Rights Act exclusively with African Americans, the law also assisted Hispanic Americans. In 1964 the Civil Rights Act was passed, making it illegal to discriminate on the basis of race, religion, sex, or national origin. Although primarily intended to safeguard the rights of African Americans, the federal law outlawed all forms of discrimination in employment, public places, and education. It also addressed voting rights and limited the use of literacy tests for the purposes of voter registration.

Although court cases and other laws banning discrimination had been passed before 1964, the Civil Rights Acts included an important provision: No federal funding would be given to any government or organization that discriminated against minorities. This sent a powerful message about the nation's vow of equal opportunity for all citizens.

Latino Leaders in Government

Latinos are represented in government at all levels, representing both political parties. The first Hispanic to serve in Congress was Joseph Marion Hernández, elected in 1822 as a delegate to the US Congress from Florida. The first Latino to serve as a US senator

JFK and The Civil Rights Act of 1964

When President John F. Kennedy addressed the nation on television on June 6, 1963, he said it was time to guarantee equal treatment of every American regardless of color. At the time, much of US society was still segregated (whites and blacks were kept apart). Congress soon began considering legislation that would address voting rights, public facilities, school desegregation, and other due rights.

Just a few months later, in November 1963, Kennedy was assassinated. Although he was never able to see his vision for a just law become a reality, Kennedy's original proposal resulted in the Civil Rights Act of 1964 just a year later. The Civil Rights Act was signed into law by President Lyndon Johnson on July 2, 1964. The legislation banned segregation in public places such as schools and swimming pools. It also made discrimination in employment and businesses illegal.[6]

President Kennedy addresses the nation on civil rights in June 1963.

was Octaviano A. Larrazolo, who served in 1928. In 1976 the Congressional Hispanic Caucus (CHC) was created. Started by five Hispanic members of Congress, the CHC sought to ensure that the needs of Hispanics were being met. Today, there are over six thousand Hispanics holding public offices.[7]

When President Bill Clinton was elected, he vowed to have a cabinet that "looked like America." Until that time, presidential cabinets were mostly composed of white men. Cabinets are important because they advise the president on important issues and policies. Under President Reagan, white men made up 85 percent of the appointments. Only one Latino, Secretary of Education Lauro Cavazos, was a member of Reagan's cabinet. Cavazos also served under George H. W. Bush, whose cabinet was 71 percent composed of white men.[8]

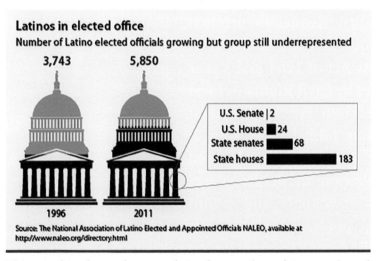

Latinos in elected office
Number of Latino elected officials growing but group still underrepresented

3,743   5,850

U.S. Senate | 2
U.S. House ▮ 24
State senates ▮ 68
State houses ▮ 183

1996   2011

Source: The National Association of Latino Elected and Appointed Officials NALEO, available at http://www.naleo.org/directory.html

This graphic shows the growth in the number of Latino elected officials from 1996 to 2011.[9]

Civil Rights Act of 1968

Intended as a follow-up to the Civil Rights Act of 1964, the Civil Rights Act of 1968 outlawed discrimination in housing practices. Also known as Title VIII or as the Fair Housing Act, it prohibits discrimination in the sale, rental, and financing of housing based on race, color, religion, sex, or national origin. Later, the law was expanded to include handicapped individuals and family status. It was signed into law on April 11, 1968, by President Lyndon Johnson just one week after the assassination of Dr. Martin Luther King Jr.

President Clinton's presidency was historic in that he appointed three Hispanics to serve on his cabinet. Federico Peña served as secretary of transportation during Clinton's first term and as secretary of energy during the second term. Clinton appointed Henry Cisneros, the former mayor of San Antonio, Texas, as secretary of housing and urban development. Aida Álvarez sat on Clinton's cabinet in her position as the administrator of the Small Business Administration. She was the first Latina and the first Puerto Rican to serve on a presidential cabinet. President Clinton also appointed Bill Richardson as the first Hispanic American to serve as the chief US delegate to the United Nations.

George W. Bush appointed two Latinos to his cabinet. Under his presidency, Alberto Gonzales became the first Hispanic to hold the office of attorney general. Bush also appointed Cuban-American businessman Carlos Gutiérrez as US secretary of commerce.

When President Barack Obama was first elected in 2008, he appointed two Hispanics to his cabinet. Mexican American Ken Salazar served as interior secretary. Hilda Solis, whose parents were from

President Bill Clinton meets with Housing Secretary Henry Cisneros (center) and other cabinet members in 1993.

Nicaragua and Mexico, was named labor secretary. In 2009 he appointed Sonia Sotomayor to the US Supreme Court, the first Hispanic justice to serve in this capacity. However, in his second term, Obama was criticized for having no Latino representation in his cabinet.

At the state level, the lack of Latino governors has been lamented, with some notable exceptions. One of the earliest was Romualdo Pacheco who was elected governor of California in 1875. More recently, Bill Richardson was elected governor of New Mexico in 2002. As more and more Latinos become elected officials, the face of the United States's political arena is changing.

The Latino Vote

Latinos turned out to vote in record numbers during the 2008 presidential election. Barack Obama and Joe Biden captured 67% of the Latino vote.[10] Four years later, Latinos helped to re-elect President Obama, giving him and Vice President Biden 71% of their votes.[11]

It is estimated that about 35 percent of Latinos are Republican and 62 percent are Democrats. But as the National Council of La Raza points out, through elections, Latinos have demonstrated that "they will support strong candidates from both major parties and that they are not tied to a single political ideology."[12] It is estimated that by 2030, the Latino voting bloc will double in size.[13] With so many Latinos going to the polls, political candidates and officials are openly

Ileana Ros-Lehtinen

Ileana Ros-Lehtinen

When Ileana Ros-Lehtinen came from Cuba at the age of seven, little did she know that one day she would become the first Latina and the first Cuban American elected to Congress. This honor came to her in 1982. As a result of her family's experience, the Republican strongly opposes the communist regime in Cuba and she works as a human rights advocate throughout the world. She has been working with other members of Congress to raise funding for the National Museum of the American Latino.

courting the Latino vote. The National Council of La Raza publishes a voter's guide that gives an overview of the issues important to Latinos. Important concerns include access to health care, education, economic opportunities, and immigration.[14] More than ever before, Latinos are involved in the political sphere and are using their votes to improve the quality of life for their communities and families.

Latinos and Schooling

"...if we are to be truly great as a nation, then we must make sure that nobody is denied an opportunity because of race, creed, or color." [1]

Robert F. Kennedy

In 1968 Mexican-American students had the highest high school dropout rate and the lowest college attendance rate in the United States.[2] At the time, many Mexican Americans were "tracked" into vocational or special education classrooms. Many believed they were incapable of a college degree. The schools that Mexican-American students attended were often run-down and poorly equipped. The students' culture was ignored in the curriculum and they were forbidden to speak Spanish in school.

The next year, as the civil rights movement was sweeping the nation, fifteen thousand Mexican-American students in East Los Angeles protested poor educational conditions by walking out of seven high schools. The students wanted to make a statement about the education that Mexican Americans were receiving. They complained that the schools were overcrowded, that they did not have any Latino teachers, that there were not enough classroom materials, and that their textbooks did not include their history or culture. While many of them had college aspirations, the vocational classes most of them were put in did not prepare them for college.

The protesters held press conferences and presented written proposals that demanded such things as fixing old buildings, having a more challenging and useful curriculum, and improving the schools' libraries. Moctesuma Esparza, a college student and community activist, and Sal Castro, one of the students' teachers, helped them organize. The walkouts, or "Chicano blowouts" as they were also called, lasted for several daysfrom March 1 to March 8, 1968.

At first, the demonstrations were peaceful. But soon the Los Angeles police force was sent out in riot gear. Orders were issued to the police to force the unarmed students back to school. Some students were arrested. Several students suffered injuries, and community leaders and parents were outraged. Esparza, Castro, and eleven others were arrested and put in jail for disturbing the peace. They became known as the "East LA 13." In addition to the educational demands, the student protesters also asked for the release of the East LA 13 and the reinstatement of Sal Castro. The situation got national attention when

César Chávez and Senator Robert Kennedy publicly supported the students and their families.

Although in the end the students did not have all their demands met, the walkouts brought attention to the educational inadequacies, and the school board eventually added more academic programs and more Latino teachers were hired. Charges against the East LA 13 were finally dropped in 1972.

Years later in 2006, Moctesuma Esparza unveiled a film he produced about the event. Called *Walkout*, the HBO film was directed by Edward James Olmos. Many of the students who participated in the walkouts later had successful careers in politics, education, and the arts. Antonio Villaraigosa, one of the student protesters, later became the mayor of Los Angeles, holding office from 2005 to 2013.

Senator Robert F. Kennedy supported the Latino community in demanding improvements in the schools.

Latinos and Schooling in the United States

For Latinos, schooling in the United States has been bittersweet. On the one hand, it has been a way for them to improve financial security for their families and attain the American dream. On the other hand, they have not always been welcome at the schoolhouse door.

Historically, Latino children have been disadvantaged in education for three reasons. First, bilingual education was not offered in the United States until the mid-1960s. Until this time, the primary method of language instruction was "sink or swim." That is, language minority students were placed in a regular classroom with little or no special instruction. Second, students whose families were migrant farm workers were refused an education because they did not have a permanent residence. Third, because of the high rates of poverty among Hispanics, many Latino children have had to work to help support their families, leading to poor academic achievement and high drop-out rates.[3]

The 2010 census reported that 63 percent of Latino students graduate from high school, 14 percent graduate from college, and only 3 percent go on to earn an advanced college degree. By comparison, 88 percent of white students finish high school, 30 percent graduate from college, and 8 percent earn advanced college degrees.[4]

A report issued in 2015 found that of all ethnic groups, Latinos have the highest high school drop-out rate—three times higher than white students and about double the rate for African-American students.[5] Research studies have shown that high school dropouts earn about $9,200 less per year than high school graduates. Those who do not complete high school are also more likely to need government assistance or serve time in prison.[6] Low educational achievement is not just bad for Latinos, but the nation as a whole.

Overturning Segregated Schools

One of the first cases to achieve educational rights for Latino students was *Méndez v. Westminster School District et al.* in 1946. The Méndez family moved to Westminster, California in 1945. Gonzalo Méndez and his wife, Felicitas, had leased forty acres in the small farming community. There were three children in the Méndez family: Sylvia, Gonzalo Jr., and Gerónimo. Like their parents, the Méndez children were all US citizens and were completely fluent in English.

One of the first things the family needed to do after their move was to register the children in the local school. Because he and his wife were busy preparing the fields, Gonzalo asked his sister, Soledad Vidaurri, to register the three Méndez children when she went to enroll her own two.

Mrs. Vidaurri had no problem registering her own two children, who did not have a Mexican-sounding last name and were light skinned. But school officials refused to enroll the Méndez children, whose last name was clearly Hispanic and who, unlike their cousins, had dark skin. The Méndez children were

Mexican-American schoolchildren in the 1940s. During this time, Hispanic students often received inferior educational services compared to those of white students.

advised to go to Hoover Elementary, "the Mexican school" a few blocks away. For years, the Orange County school system had been segregated on the grounds that Mexican children were "more poorly clothed and mentally inferior to white children."[7]

Infuriated, Gonzalo Méndez contacted attorney David C. Marcus. Marcus had made a name for himself by successfully challenging whites-only public facilities in *López v. Seccombe*. Just tried the year before, *López v. Seccombe* ensured that all people would have equal access to public pools and parks. Ignacio López, a US citizen who lived in San Bernadino, California, was outraged that he and other Mexican Americans were not allowed to use the public swimming pool. López had served in World War II and was a graduate of the University of Southern California. Citing the Fourteenth Amendment of the US Constitution, Marcus argued that the city had to open public swimming pools to all its citizens. The judge ruled in López's favor and issued a court order.

When Marcus heard the Méndez's story, he took the case on and filed a lawsuit on the family's behalf. The trial took place in July 1945 over the course of two weeks. The actual court order, however, was not delivered until February 1946. The judge ruled that a public school education must be available to all children, regardless of their ethnic origin. *Méndez v. Westminster School District et al.* went on to influence the famous Supreme Court case *Brown v. The Board of Education of Topeka, Kansas*, which outlawed racial segregation in public schools.[8]

The Bilingual Education Acts

The Bilingual Education Act of 1968 was the first law at the national level that provided extra funding to school districts to meet the special needs of Spanish-language students. A year after the law was passed, $7.5 million was slated for bilingual education programs. The funds could be used for training teachers to work with language minority students, to develop materials that could be used by English language learners, and for programs that involved parents in schooling.

But proponents worried that because the Bilingual Education Act was voluntary, it would not be employed as intended. To ensure compliance, amendments to the law were passed in 1974 as a result of a groundbreaking court case in California.

The case was a class action suit against the San Francisco Unified School District. A class action suit is a lawsuit by one or more people on behalf of a large group of people with the same interest or issue. Chinese-American students there protested that they were not receiving an equal education because of their limited English skills. At first, the lower courts ruled that the Chinese students were receiving a quality education. But when it reached the Supreme Court, the justices reversed the decision by a unanimous ruling. The justices wrote: "There is no equality of treatment by providing students with the same facilities, textbooks, teachers and curriculum, for students who do not understand English are effectively foreclosed from any meaningful education."[9]

The ruling of the case led to a federal mandate that all school districts take actions to correct educational issues for students whose native language was not English. For Latinos, the landmark decision meant that schools had to ensure that classroom instruction was meaningful for all students, including English language learners.

Another important court case was *Castañeda v. Pickard*. This 1981 case involved Mexican-American children in the Raymondville Independent School District in Texas. Parents charged that the teaching practices used in schools violated their children's rights. They argued that the school district did not offer bilingual education programs that helped minority students. They also charged that because school officials used "ability tracking" to group students, it caused the segregation of Hispanic students.

The Fifth Circuit Court of Appeals agreed with the Mexican-American families. The case established standards for the education of English language learners, including having qualified educators. This meant that school districts had to hire new staff in some cases and train current staff to make sure they were meeting students' needs.

Educational Challenges

Not all court cases or legislation have been in support of bilingual education. Proposition 227 was passed in 1998 to end bilingual education in California. It was passed by voters by a margin of 61 percent to 39 percent. The law calls for a program to intensively teach children English as soon as they enter school. The law stated:

> Whereas, the English language is the national public language of the United States; and young immigrant children can easily acquire full fluency in a new language if they are heavily exposed to that language . . . It is resolved that: all children in California public schools shall be taught English as rapidly and effectively as possible (Proposition 227, Article I, 1998).[10]

Critics of Proposition 227 said that the law was racist and was antibilingual education. They argued

Author Ron Unz was a proponent of the proposal to end bilingual education in California.

that English immersion could be cruel, not effective, and was unrealistic in terms of the time expectations it takes to learn English.

Many also feel that the No Child Left Behind (NCLB) law, passed in 2001, hurt Latino students. By focusing on literacy, NCLB sought to improve school achievement and hold schools accountable for it. From the onset, the law was controversial because of its emphasis on testing and the threat of withholding federal funding for underperforming schools. But because many Latinos do not do as well on these tests, they are often held back a grade or not allowed to graduate because of poor scores. Some feel that many of these standardized tests are loaded with bias. Not being fluent in English can certainly have a negative impact on a student's scores. Not being familiar with American culture and expressions can also result in lower scores.

In 2009 the Obama administration announced the Race to the Top contest, pledging $4 billion to improve K-12 education. But controversy followed when it was revealed that funding would depend on states adopting national curriculum standards. And because schools would have to show growth based, in part, on students' test scores, some teachers' unions, school administrators, and parent groups called the high-stakes testing unfair.

Educators point out that bias against Latinos continues to be evident in the school curriculum and in textbooks. The curriculum is what students study and when they do so during their schooling. If students do not see their culture and history reflected in the curriculum, it may result in disinterest and lower academic achievement. Textbooks also need to reflect the many cultures that make up the population. However, school texts do not always do that. Some educational researchers argue that Latinos are regularly omitted from both the school curriculum and from school textbooks.[11]

Affirmative Action

Affirmative action refers to a policy or a program that seeks to eliminate discrimination in education (and employment) against minorities. Many colleges, for example, try to ensure a diverse student body by having special programs to admit ethnic minorities, especially in underrepresented majors or professions.

In 1978, affirmative action was challenged in the case of the University of *California Regents v. Allan Bakke.* Bakke was a student trying to gain admission to the medical school at the University of California, Davis. After he was denied entry for the second time, he claimed that he was the victim of "reverse discrimination." He argued that minority candidates were not held to the same entrance standards (GPAs, test scores, etc.) that white students were expected to have. Bakke sued the California university system. The California Supreme Court ruled in Bakke's favor, 8–1. The university system appealed and in 1978 the case was heard before the US Supreme Court.

In their 5–4 decision, the US Supreme Court justices were sharply divided. The court ruled that racial quotas could no longer be used in school admissions. A quota is a limited or fixed number. Racial quotas in education involve a system that ensures that a specific number of people from certain minority groups be admitted. However, the Court did stipulate that race could still be considered in student admissions.

For Latinos, the *Bakke* decision was devastating. Latino organizations worried that the effect of *Bakke* would be to resegregate American campuses. While most schools did not use the *Bakke* case to exclude minorities, some did, and there have been recent challenges to affirmative action. LULAC has strongly opposed such measures. The LULAC president at the time, Hector Flores said, "LULAC firmly believes that the continuation of affirmative action is a number one priority and is essential to maintaining a diverse student body at our nation's top colleges and universities reflective of the racial and ethnic makeup of our great country, a country of opportunities."[12] Supporters of affirmative action point out that the policy is not meant to replace qualified whites with unqualified minorities. Rather, it is meant to improve equity and access for all.

Another important case in the issue of affirmative action is *Hopwood v. University of Texas*. In 1992 Cheryl Hopwood was denied admission to the University of Texas Law School. Hopwood, who is white, sued the university maintaining that she was better qualified than some of the minority candidates who had already been admitted. When the trial went

Protesters voice their displeasure with the *Bakke* decision, which ruled that specific racial quotas could not be used in college admissions.

to court in 1994, the judge ruled in favor of the university, stating that affirmative action programs were still needed because racism was still part of our society.

Hopwood appealed, and in 1996 the Fifth Circuit Court overturned the lower court's decision, saying that the university's race-sensitive admission policy could not be used to increase student diversity at the school. The university appealed the decision to the US Supreme Court, though the Court declined to hear the case.

Affirmative Action on the Ballot

In 1996 Proposition 209 was passed in the state of California with a 54% vote. Generally seen as an anti-affirmative action law, Proposition 209 prohibited public institutions to use race, ethnicity, or gender in decision making. Public outcry was immediate and a number of organizations, such as the American Civil Liberties Union and the Feminist Majority, issued public statements condemning the measure. Since Proposition 209's passage, there have also been a number of lawsuits challenging it, but it has not been overturned.

Ten years later, a law modeled on Proposition 209 was passed in Michigan. The law prohibited preferential treatment of minority groups in public institutions. It was challenged in the 6th Circuit Court of Appeals and the case was eventually heard by the US Supreme Court in 2014. In a 6–2 ruling, the Court upheld the law as constitutional, saying that states had the right to ban the practice of affirmative action through public voting.

Spanish and the English-Only Movement

Language is of central concern in many of the controversies surrounding the education of Latinos. For many Latinos, Spanish continues to be the main language spoken in the home. While this fluency in another language can be a source of opportunity, it can also pose challenges in school, at work, and in politics.

Thirty states have officially declared English to be their official language. For example, in 1986, 73% of California voters agreed to make English the state's official language. Seventy-four percent of Arizona's voters supported a similar law in 2006. And nearly 76% of Oklahoma's voters supported an amendment that made English the official language of the state in 2010.

Plyler v. Doe

Are children who are born outside the United States and enter the country illegally with their parents allowed to attend American public schools? According to *Plyler v. Doe* (1982), yes. In a 5 to 4 decision, the Supreme Court ruled that under the Fourteenth Amendment, a state cannot deny school enrollment to children of illegal immigrants. In the majority decision, the Court reasoned that illegal immigrants and their children—although not citizens of the United States—are people "in any ordinary sense of the term" and, therefore, are protected by the Fourteenth Amendment of the US Constitution.

A number of "English-only" political groups have also tried to make English the only official language across the United States. [13]

The English-only movement has affected Latinos in a number of ways. Many Latinos feel that the English-only movement is an indication of anti-immigrant sentiment. They point out that with each successive generation, immigrants learn English and become absorbed into mainstream American culture. They argue that in Puerto Rico, both Spanish and English are official languages, to no ill effect.

Even though Spanish may not be an official language and it has been challenged aggressively, it remains the second most frequently used language in the United States.

Ethnic Studies

Growing out of the civil rights movement, ethnic studies is an interdisciplinary field popular on many high school and college campuses. It combines history, anthropology, literature, and other disciplines to study the histories, cultures, and languages of ethnic minority peoples in the United States. The 1960s saw the establishment of academic centers devoted to Asian American, African American, Native American, and Latino American studies.

But critics argue that because ethnic studies examines American history through a critical lens, these courses are anti-American and can lead to hostility between groups. Some colleges have reduced funding or completely eliminated their ethnic studies programs, citing budget cuts.

Ethnic studies has also been challenged at the K-12 level. In 2010 the Arizona legislature banned Ethnic Studies from the public school curriculum. According to the law, school districts that did not comply would not receive public funds. In 2012 the Tucson Unified School District in Arizona ended Mexican-American studies to avoid losing more than $1 million a month in state public school funds. After public outcry, the school district reintroduced an elective Mexican-American Studies course for college credit. Legislators in California are similarly finding alternate ways to offer ethnic studies courses in secondary schools.[14]

The DREAM Act

Every year, approximately sixty-five thousand undocumented students graduate from high school in the United States. But because they do not have legal status, they cannot go to college or trade school because they are not eligible for grants, loans, scholarships, or legal jobs. In 2001 a proposal was introduced in the US Senate to grant undocumented students

The DREAM Act proposed that residency status be given to undocumented students. The proposal did not receive the needed support and was not enacted on the national level.

residency status and be able to attend an institution of higher education. Called the Development, Relief, and Education for Alien Minors (DREAM) Act, the legislation has been met with controversy, failing to pass at the national level. Although supporters point out the positive economic and social impact the law would have, critics argue that the law would encourage illegal immigration.

Some states, such as California, Texas, and New York, have adopted their own versions of the DREAM Act. By being recognized as state residents, Latinos applying to the program qualify for lower in-state tuition and for financial aid.

Hope for the Future

Parents and educators realize that succeeding in school and earning high school and college degrees are critical for a good life. To promote educational success, a number of programs have been developed with Latino students in mind.

At the K-12 school level, some magnet and charter schools are targeting Latino students and providing curricular materials that emphasize Latino contributions. Special instruction is also being offered to those students who do not do well on standardized tests. To combat the high drop-out rate for Latino high school students, incentive programs have been established that reward students for good grades and school attendance. The Race to the Top Fund seeks to turn around low-achieving schools and recruit and retain

Today many programs are being instituted with the goal of helping Latino children succeed in school.

the most effective teachers, especially in low-income communities.[15]

In 2005 the High School Initiative was launched at the federal level, aiming to combat the high drop-out rate, improve teacher quality, and promote college awareness. The program recognizes the grim educational situation for Latino students. It promises to provide more resources "to those Hispanic students who are most at-risk of dropping out."[16] Critics, however, say that the plan requires more standardized testing and that the funds are coming from budget cuts in other educational areas.

With the cost of college in the United States averaging thirty thousand dollars per year,[17] one major stumbling block for prospective Latino college students has been the high cost of attending. Many Latino students qualify for financial aid, however. While the Higher Education Act (HEA) was signed into effect in 1965 by President Lyndon B. Johnson, it has lost funding in recent years. This act established the guaranteed student loan program, making financial aid available to all college students who need it. However, many community leaders charge that the program's budget has been slashed drastically, and not all who qualify receive appropriate aid. Other important sources of financial support are the Hispanic Scholarship Fund and the Gates Millennium Scholars Program, allowing many Latino students to complete their college degrees.

Another obstacle for Mexican-American students has been lack of knowledge about applying to and attending college. One University of Georgia program, *Vamos a la Universidad* (Let's Go to College), targets bilingual students. Students participate in the program during the summer between the end of middle school and their freshman year in high school. These students have a college mindset, and many of them will be the first in their families to attend college. *Vamos a la Universidad* tries to simplify the process of applying to, attending, and graduating from college. Program staffer Nadia Madrid reflects on her own background: "We all have different experiences in getting into college. None of my family went to college and I didn't know how to do it."[18] The nonprofit College Board publishes in English and Spanish to help students and their families gain access to higher education.

Through free, online programs like Big Future and annual conferences such as Prepárate, the College Board seeks to increase Latino college enrollment and completion rates.[19]

Latinos value education and recognize its importance in life success. With the renewed attention that educational issues are receiving, it is hoped that the next generation of Latino students will be the best educated thus far.

Latino Immigration

Talissa Carrasco had dreams of attending law school. A native of Peru, she was attending the University of California at Davis even though she was an undocumented immigrant. Without legal residence, Talissa could not get a driver's license or a job to help pay for her school.

To help young people like Talissa, in 2012 President Obama announced a new policy called the Deferred Action for Childhood Arrivals (DACA). DACA would protect undocumented young people who came to the United States as children from deportation. They would also be eligible to receive a renewable two-year work permit.

Talissa applied, met all the requirements, and was granted DACA status. "Now that I have DACA," Talissa said, "I feel like I have a sense of security. I can get a job that will help me pay for school and feel that I no longer need to hide my identity from the world."[1]

Immigration Controversy

While the United States prides itself on being a nation of immigrants, the issue has been a source of controversy since the beginning of the twentieth century. As millions of immigrants entered the United States through Ellis Island in New York, they were met with a mixed reception. On the one hand, they were welcomed for the richness of cultures and the ready pool of labor they brought. On the other hand, they were rejected for their different customs, languages, and jobs they accepted for very low wages.

In 1924 the US Congress passed the Immigration Act of 1924. This act established strict quotas based on country of origin. Immigrants had to apply for visas, pay special fees, and pass certain tests. There was an anti-immigrant feeling in the nation. Through this act the US Border Patrol was also created.

During the Great Depression of the 1930s, most citizens felt the effects of the severe economic decline that was impacting the entire world. In the United States, many people lost their jobs and their homes. As people used up their savings, charities struggled to provide the basic necessities for millions of suddenly poor families. Soup kitchens that offered simple but nutritious meals to the needy were set up in many towns.

For Latinos, the Great Depression was especially devastating. In addition to the economic impact on their families, they also suffered increased prejudice. Although in most cases Latinos had been born and raised in the United States, some Anglos viewed them as foreigners who were taking away much-needed jobs. Mexican Americans in particular were subjected to harassment and intimidation. Approximately five hundred thousand Mexican Americans were encouraged or forced to leave the country.[2]

But the tide turned after World War II when workers again were in short supply. In 1942 the US government entered into an agreement with the Mexican government to supply temporary workers, known as braceros, for agricultural work. Under this program, an estimated five million Mexicans were allowed to enter and work in the United States until 1964, when the program was discontinued.

On October 3, 1965, President Lyndon B. Johnson signed into law the Immigration and Nationality Act. This legislation ended the national origin immigration quotas that had been in place in the United States since the Immigration Act of 1924. The elimination of national origin quotas helped Latino immigrants. However, later legislation has hurt immigration policy for Latinos.

Although the yearly limit of immigrants from any one country is twenty thousand, it is estimated that between eleven million and twelve million people are in the United States illegally.[3] About seven million of these undocumented immigrants are employed in mostly low-level jobs such as construction, food processing, and housekeeping. While some people argue that they are taking away jobs from legal residents of the United States, others argue that without their labor, the US economy could not function.

Although there are quotas restricting how many people can immigrate to the United States from a given country, refugees have special consideration. A refugee is a person fleeing persecution in his or her homeland. According to US immigration law, refugees are in a special category that is not subject to immigration quotas. Refugees are granted permission to live and work in the United States and are eligible to receive financial assistance from the government. Examples of refugees are people who have been political prisoners, human rights activists, and people whose religion is discriminated against in their home country. Latin-American refugees include immigrants from Chile, Cuba, Nicaragua, and El Salvador.

In 1986 Congress passed the Simpson-Mazzoli Act. The act specified that anyone who could prove that he or she had been in the country for five years could be granted citizenship. However, fewer people applied for citizenship than expected and many immigrants, especially those from Mexico, continue to live in the United States without permission and without the basic rights of American citizens. The law also stated that American businessmen who knowingly hired these undocumented citizens could be arrested or fined.

Until 2003, the Immigration and Naturalization Service (INS) was the primary agency in the United States that dealt with immigration issues. Today, the agency is officially called the US Citizenship and

Immigration Services (USCIS) and is part of the Department of Homeland Security.

"Illegal alien" was the term most commonly used for those entering the United States without permission. The term refers to any person who enters and lives in the United States without permission. Because of the term's negative associations, "unauthorized resident" and "undocumented worker" are now more commonly used.

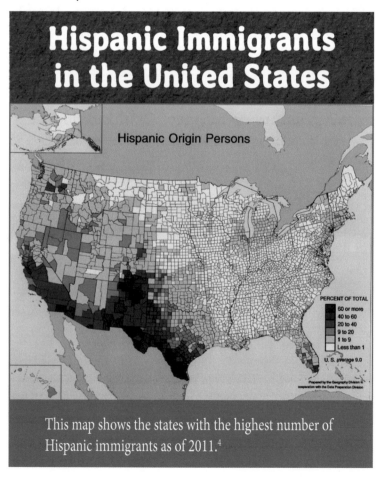

Hispanic Immigrants in the United States

Hispanic Origin Persons

PERCENT OF TOTAL
- 60 or more
- 40 to 60
- 20 to 40
- 9 to 20
- 1 to 9
- Less than 1

U. S. average 9.0

This map shows the states with the highest number of Hispanic immigrants as of 2011.[4]

The Border Patrol

In 1924 the US Congress approved the creation of the Border Patrol. The Border Patrol intercepts people trying to enter the United States illegally. From the beginning, the Border Patrol was caught up in controversy.

Today the Border Patrol uses all kinds of sophisticated methods for its monitoring. Movement sensors, night vision goggles, and helicopters are just some of the equipment they use. The Border Patrol captures about one million people each year at the United States–Mexico border. In recent years, the Border Patrol has increased its surveillance along Florida's coasts.

There have also been a number of court cases involving the Border Patrol. One of the more scandalous ones involved high school football coach Benjamin Murillo. Coach Murillo worked at Bowie High School in El Paso, Texas, a town that is on the Mexico–Texas border. Mexican-American Murillo, who was a US citizen and was wearing a Bowie High School football coaching shirt and shorts, was stopped by the Border Patrol. While one agent pointed a gun to his head, another agent searched his car.

When word spread of the incident, the staff and student body at Bowie High decided to take action. Many of them had also been stopped, questioned, and harassed by Border Patrol agents. Seven of them filed a class action suit, with Coach Murillo serving as the lead plaintiff.

In El Paso, Texas, in 2011, Bowie High School football coach Robert Padilla points out where a shooting occurred across the border a few hundred feet from the school as students practiced.

In 1992 the case was decided by a US district court, which found that the Border Patrol had violated the Fourth and Fifth Amendments of the Constitution. The Fourth Amendment of the Bill of Rights protects people from unreasonable searches. The Fifth Amendment guards citizens' legal rights. The judge said that the high school "provided an oasis of safety and freedom for the students and staff" and that the continued harassment by the El Paso Border Patrol was "both an invasion of their civil rights and the oasis."[5]

As a direct result of the Bowie High School case, the Border Patrol took steps to establish complaint procedures, bilingual complaint forms, and a toll-free telephone number where complaints could be logged. The English-Spanish hotline number is now displayed on all Border Patrol vehicles.

The Rio Grande (Spanish for "Big River") provides a natural border between Mexico and Texas and New Mexico. Those who cross the Río Grande are sometimes referred to negatively as "wetbacks." These immigrants often hire people called coyotes. Coyotes are paid to smuggle immigrants into the United States.

In 1904 the United States began patrolling the border with Mexico. Large numbers of Mexicans began crossing into the United States during the Mexican Revolution (1910–1917). The conflict caused many Mexicans to flee their homeland in search of safety. As hundreds of thousands of people came to the United States, Congress approved the creation of the Border Patrol in 1924.

By 1953 the Border Patrol had caught more than 865,000 people. The US government felt pressured to stem the flow of immigration. In 1954 Operation Wetback was launched. Although the goal of this campaign was to capture and deport illegal immigrants, it openly focused on Mexicans in general. Close to four million people of Mexican heritage were deported.

Some of the immigrants were sent back to their homelands along with their children who had been born in the United States and, by law, were American citizens. Throughout the Southwest, police arrested citizens in raids that targeted Mexican Americans.

Some Mexican Americans left the United States on their own as the raids increased.[6]

By many accounts, the immigration officials used a heavy hand in enforcing the law. They questioned any citizen that they thought was "Mexican-looking." Their unfair practices angered many Americans who protested to the government. Operation Wetback was eventually abandoned.

Immigration from Central and South America

Many immigrants from Central and South America seeking a better life attempt to enter the United States through Mexico. People from Guatemala, Honduras, El Salvador, and other Latin-American countries resort to the services of the coyotes to help them enter the United States. The human smugglers got their name from their ability to move stealthily at night, evading law enforcement. Coyotes have some defenders, who say that they are a sort of Underground Railroad, helping poor people find jobs and rescuing refugees from persecution. But many others say that the opposite is true and point to the hundreds of deaths the coyotes cause each year.

Because what coyotes are doing is illegal, they take many deadly risks. Every year, hundreds of immigrants die from dehydration, hunger, and heatstroke—often when they are abandoned by coyotes in the middle of a desert. Others die when their overloaded vans and trucks crash, killing those on board.

Border Patrol agents detain an illegal immigrant. The agency has been under fire for its treatment of Mexicans.

The number of immigrants trying to enter the country, and the abuses they often endure, have led some states, like Arizona, to pass "anti-coyote laws." Under this legislation, those who engage in human trafficking are subject to fines and can be jailed. The law is not without critics, however. Some people fear that the immigrants themselves will be prosecuted under this law. When Arizona's top prosecutor wanted to use the law to charge fifty-one undocumented immigrants with a felony, Senator Timothy Bee, who sponsored the legislation, said, "The law was designed to go after those who are involved in drug trafficking and human trafficking for a profit."[7] How the law is applied and enforced continues to be a source of debate and controversy.

Anyone entering or leaving the United States is required to pass through a customs checkpoint like the one seen here at the Mexico border.

Immigration From the Caribbean

For immigrants from the Caribbean, entry to the United States is often by means of watercraft. The crossing is dangerous and many die at sea trying to get to the United States.

Many Dominicans travel to nearby Puerto Rico from where they can take a flight to the United States. Because one does not need a passport to travel from Puerto Rico to the United States, many of them enter the country that way. Tragedy often ensues, however, when Dominicans sail on the channel between the two islands. The relatively narrow eighty-mile-wide Mona Passage is rough and shark-filled. Many Dominicans are intercepted by the Border Patrol and returned to their homeland. Others die when their boats capsize.

Puerto Ricans who come to the US mainland are not considered immigrants since they are US citizens. Even though there is a small minority of Puerto Ricans who favor independent status, polls show that the majority prefer continued commonwealth status. The majority points out that this status provides stability.

Cuban immigrants are often given special consideration because of their political status. The Mariel

The Special Case of Puerto Ricans

While Puerto Ricans are US citizens, many of them choose to emigrate from the island. The "Great Migration" of Puerto Ricans to the United States began right after World War II. Most of these migrants made their way to New York City. Many of them settled in the area known as Spanish Harlem. This population led to the term "Nuyorican," a blending of New York and Puerto Rican. In 1998 New York City mayor Rudolph Giuliani declared June 7 through June 14 as Puerto Rican Week in the city.

Boatlift of 1980 brought focus to the situation in Cuba and Cuban refugees status in the United States. In 1980 the social and economic climate in Cuba was dismal. To relieve pressure, Cuban leader Fidel Castro announced he would allow anyone to leave the island nation out of the port of Mariel. Thousands of boats arrived from the United States and anchored in the Cuban port to transport family and friends back to the United States. From April to September when the port was open, 125,000 Cubans fled the island. Many of the boats turned out to be unseaworthy. Twenty-seven people died en route to Florida.

When the Cuban refugees arrived in Miami, authorities were unprepared for the large number of people. Makeshift refugee camps could not meet the demands of the migrants. Although many of them

Immigrants arrive in the United States in boats from Cuba.

were released soon upon arrival, many others were detained and sent to other processing centers in Pennsylvania, Wisconsin, and Arkansas. As weeks turned into months, many detainees protested, claiming that they were being unfairly held in the camps.

Rumors began to circulate that Castro had loaded the boats with criminals and mental hospital patients. This led to an anti-immigrant sentiment in the United States. Eventually, the Marielitos became part of American society, many of whom have worked to bring other Cubans to the United States.

More recently, the controversial "wet foot/dry foot" policy has faced scrutiny. Under the policy, refugees who reach US soil are allowed to stay, but those stopped at sea are returned to their native countries. In 2006 the Hernández family left Cuba in the middle of the night. After being at sea for three days, they finally spotted land. The rickety boat had reached the Florida Keys just as the boat began to fall apart. The family made it to an abandoned bridge that no longer connected to land. The new bridge, which does connect to dry land, was just a hundred yards away.

As the refugees clung to the pilings, they were spotted by the US Coast Guard. The Coast Guard had been instructed to enforce the "wet foot/dry foot" policy. The Coast Guard decided that the former bridge was not part of American soil because sections of the bridge were missing and it no longer connected to dry land. Therefore, Coast Guard officials did not think the bridge counted as "dry land." Human rights leaders were outraged, saying that returning the

Rámon Saúl Sánchez rests during his 2006 hunger strike protesting the return of refugees to Cuba by US authorities.

refugees to Cuba was cruel and that they would be persecuted if returned to the island.

Ramón Saúl Sánchez, head of the Cuban-American Democracy Movement, went on an eleven-day hunger strike to protest the group's return to Cuba. He and others argued that the Cubans would be treated poorly if they were sent back to their homeland.

On February 28, 2006, a federal judge ruled that the US government had acted illegally when it sent home the fifteen Cubans who had made it to the bridge. Further, the judge ordered federal officials to

Hispanic Immigrants in the United States

U.S. Hispanic Population Growth, by Country of Origin, 2000-2010

	POPULATION		GROWTH	
	2010	2000	Number	%
All Hispanics	**50,478**	**35,306**	**15,172**	**43.0**
Guatemalan	1,044	372	672	180.3
Salvadoran	1,649	655	994	151.7
Colombian	909	471	438	93.1
Dominican	1,415	765	650	84.9
Mexican	31,798	20,641	11,158	54.1
Cuban	1,786	1,242	544	43.8
Puerto Rican	4,624	3,406	1,218	35.7

Notes: Hispanic population growth among country of origin groups with a population of 900,000 or more in 2010. Growth rates are computed from unrounded data.

Source: 2010 Census and 2000 Census (Ennis, Ríos-Vargas and Albert, 2011)

PEW RESEARCH CENTER

There has been a large jump in the number of Hispanic immigrants living in the United States since 2000.

"use their best efforts" to help the Cubans return to the United States.[8]

Immigration Today

One of the more controversial immigration policies has been the Illegal Immigration Reform and Immigrant Responsibility Act of 1996. It is sometimes referred to as "IIRAIRA" for short. Under the law, people could be deported for crimes that had occurred long ago or even for relatively minor offenses, such as shoplifting. The law also gives the right to law enforcement agencies to detain people until they are deported. The law applies even to permanent residents who marry American citizens or who have children born in the United States.

The law was tested in 1998 when Jesús Collado, a permanent resident of the United States, who had lived in New York for twenty-four years, was arrested at Kennedy Airport when returning from his homeland of the Dominican Republic. He was put in jail and told he would be deported back to the Dominican Republic for a misdemeanor crime he had committed in 1974.

Collado's case attracted nationwide attention. During the months that Collado was in jail, he was denied permission to visit his wife and three children, two of whom suffered serious health problems. Supporters argued that the law was unfair and was being applied too harshly. After serving seven months in jail, Judge Douglas B. Schoppert of the New York Immigration Court dismissed the case against Collado

Hispanics in Los Angeles, California, participate in a march to protest illegal immigration reform by the US Congress in 2007.

and he was released. The US Supreme Court further interpreted the law, concluding that Congress had not intended for IIRAIRA to be applied to people who committed a past crime if that crime would not have been a deportable offense at the time.

After the September 11 attacks, immigration policy was again under scrutiny. Many felt that foreign-born terrorists were taking advantage of the United States' too-lax immigration policy. While much of the anti-immigrant sentiment was directed at Middle Easterners, Latinos were also condemned.

By 2006 discussion on immigration reached a feverish pitch. As debates regarding immigration raged in Congress, protests, demonstrations, and public meetings focused on the issue. The nation became further divided when "*Nuestro Himno*" (Our Anthem), a Spanish-language recording of "The Star-Spangled Banner" was released on April 28, 2006. It featured singers such as Haitian-born Wyclef Jean, Cuban-American rapper Pitbull, Mexican pop star Gloria Trevi, and Puerto Rican singers Carlos Ponce and Olga Tañón.

Controversy immediately ensued over the Spanish-language version. Critics pointed out that "*Nuestro Himno*" is not an exact translation and that some of the phrases and war references were completely omitted. Charles Key, Francis Scott Key's great-great-grandson, charged that the Spanish version is unpatriotic and declared that the national anthem should be sung only in English. He said, "I think it's a despicable thing that someone is going into our society from another country and . . . changing our national anthem."[9] President George W. Bush voiced his discontent with the song saying, "I think people who want to be a citizen of this country ought to learn English and they ought to learn to sing the national anthem in English."[10]

Latinos responded by saying that, as it is with all musical translations, it is impossible to do a literal translation and keep the rhyme and melody intact. Their rendition, they countered, was patriotic and respectful. Adam Kidron, the British music executive who had the original idea for the Spanish-language version, said: "It has the passion, it has the respect, it has all of the things that you really want an anthem to have and it carries the melody."[11]

The Immigration Debate Continues

In May 2006 President George W. Bush announced that six thousand additional Border Patrol officers would be sent to the United States–Mexico border to help stop undocumented immigrants coming into the United States illegally each year. As part of the same $1.9 billion immigration reform plan, President Bush promised to help legal immigrants attain US citizenship. He said, "We are a nation of laws, and we must enforce our laws. We are also a nation of immigrants, and we must uphold that tradition, which has strengthened our country in so many ways."[12]

About one hundred students walked out of classes at Tyler High School in Tyler, Texas, on March 31, 2006, to protest a proposed congressional crackdown on illegal immigration.

By and large, most Latinos support immigration. They point out that the United States is known as a country of immigrants and that this cultural heritage has strengthened the country. Not all Latinos are in favor of immigration, however. Some argue that increased entry of undocumented workers leads to lower wages for everyone. Union leader César Chávez, for example, rallied against illegal immigration by pointing out that undocumented workers are often willing to work for less than the minimum wage. These laborers, desperate for work, would often break the United Farm Workers strikes.

Despite all the controversy associated with immigration, some surveys show that Americans' views of immigrants are less negative today than they have been in the past. Further, those who have contact with immigrants are more positive.[13]

Chapter 7

Latino Workers

"I think organized labor is a necessary part of democracy. Organized labor is the only way to have fair distribution of wealth." [1]

—Labor leader and activist Dolores Huerta

Latinos have been a part of the US workforce since the very beginnings of the nation. Many of the earliest business owners and laborers worked in the livestock industry. Cattle, sheep, and horses were important parts of the economy in the New World and colonial America.

As the United States expanded into the West, Mexicans were vital in homesteading, cattle driving, and laying down the railways. In the South and East, Hispanics worked in a number of American cities. Cuban *tabaqueros* (tobacco workers) worked in Key West and Ybor City, Florida, which became known as Cigar City, USA. In Boston's South End, many Puerto Ricans were factory and farm workers.

One of the first things Latinos did to help themselves was to set up mutual aid societies. These *mutualistas* help members by pooling resources and then assisting individuals through loans, housing, and help finding jobs. These societies also had a social function in that they helped during births and funerals, and hosted dances and other social events. Mutualistas were especially popular in the first half of the 20th century.

By the 1900s much of the agricultural work in the United States was being done by Mexican migrants. They provided a ready labor force for American agriculture. The Mexican Revolution of 1910 pushed thousands of fearful and desperate Mexicans over the border in search of food and work.

The Ludlow Massacre

In 1913 a tragedy at John D. Rockefeller's Colorado Fuel and Oil Company involved many Latino workers and their families. The miners working there were tired of the poor working conditions and wages. While Rockefeller and other industrialists were getting richer and richer, workers did not seem to be benefiting from company profits. Living and working in Ludlow, Colorado, they were completely dependent on the company store, doctors, and law enforcement.

The United Mine Workers Association began organizing the miners. They presented their demands to the company asking for, among other things, safer working conditions, fairer wages, and the right to choose their own boardinghouses and doctors. When

Tent camps set up by striking mine workers in Ludlow, Colorado, were attacked by company guards in 1914.

the company refused their demands, the miners decided to strike on September 23, 1913. The strikers were immediately evicted from the company housing and they were forced to set up tents.

At first, the company was able to hire "scabs," nonunion replacement workers. But as the striking miners harassed the scabs for working, the company had a hard time keeping employees. Despite the harsh winter, the strikers refused to give in. Company guards were sent to intimidate the strikers. The guards cruised the tent colony with the "Death Special," an armored car mounted with a machine gun. The miners soon dug pits under the tents so that their families could seek shelter from the bullets that were shot indiscriminately at the tents.

On April 20, 1914, the company guards, along with state militia, shot at the tents and then burned them down. Twenty people, including two women and eleven children, were killed. Half of those killed were Mexican Americans. To retaliate, miners in nearby towns rioted, destroying mines and killing mine guards. Only when President Woodrow Wilson intervened and sent the US Army was order restored. Although Rockefeller refused to negotiate an agreement, the event did cause companies to consider using negotiating strategies instead of confrontation.

Years later, folk singer Woody Guthrie immortalized the events in his song "Ludlow Massacre." Although Ludlow is no longer inhabited, a granite monument stands at the site of the massacre. Known as the Ludlow Tent Colony, it is a National Register of Historic Places site. Archaeologists continue to excavate the site and have found tent platforms, cellars, and artifacts related to daily life in the colony as well as from the day of the massacre.[2] The incident is a sobering event in the history of American workers.

Braceros, Maquiladoras, and Operation Bootstrap

Both world wars stimulated the US economy, and demand for labor grew dramatically. During World War II, the United States was in dire need

A memorial service is held in honor of those killed in the 1914 Ludlow Massacre.

of agricultural workers. That need resulted in the Emergency Farm Labor Program in 1942, commonly called the Bracero Program. *Brazo* is the Spanish word for "arm"; a *bracero* is a manual laborer. The Bracero Program was an agreement between the United States and Mexico that allowed Mexicans to enter the United States for the purpose of working on farms and railroads. An estimated five million Mexicans worked in the United States under this program until 1964 when it was discontinued. While the program provided much needed employment for the Mexican workers, the braceros endured racism as well as difficult living and working conditions. Because the work contracts were in English, the braceros did not fully understand their rights or conditions of employment. When the contracts expired, the braceros were required to return to their homeland. Lee G. Williams, the US Department of Labor official who had been in charge of the program, described it as a system of "legalized slavery."[3]

As the Bracero Program was phased out, another labor program known as *maquiladoras* was started. Maquiladoras are factories in which goods are

These Mexicans were bean pickers under the Bracero Program in the 1940s.

produced or assembled under a special program that allows the factory owners to pay little or no taxes. Maquiladoras along the United States–Mexican border employ thousands of mostly Mexican female workers. Lured by the prospect of work, hundreds of thousands of Mexicans have immigrated to these border towns. They get paid much lower wages than their US counterparts. Although initially intended to fill the labor need of workers unemployed by the end of the Bracero Program, today most of the maquiladora workers are female.

Another program that impacted Latinos was Operation Bootstrap. The English expression of "pulling oneself up by one's own bootstraps" implies that one betters oneself by one's own efforts. It was a program started in Puerto Rico in 1947 that sought to reduce poverty by increasing industry. US companies were lured to the island by low import duties, freedom from taxation, and a desperate workforce. Puerto Rico's economy shifted from agriculture to manufacturing and service industries. At first, it was hailed as an economic miracle. But as time went by, many felt that the only change that the program had brought about was that the formerly poor agricultural workers had merely become poor city workers.

Latino Workers Unite

Latinos have also organized into workers' unions. Latino workers laboring under unsafe conditions and below minimum wage formed unions to demand changes of their employers. These organized groups have been important in obtaining higher wages, health care benefits, and safer working conditions. Today, about 10 percent of union members are Latino.[4] In 2004 UNITE (Union of Needletrades, Textiles and Industrial Employees) and HERE (Hotel Employees and Restaurant Employees) merged to form UNITE HERE. The organization has close to one million members, many of them Latino.

Another policy that has helped Latinos in the workforce has been affirmative action. Affirmative action is a series of laws and policies that seek to stop discrimination for certain groups. It can involve quotas, a certain minimum number of people admitted into a program or hired in a particular job. Critics, however, say that affirmative action unfairly keeps more qualified applicants out of jobs and disadvantages nonminorities.

The Civil Rights Act of 1964 was also instrumental in helping Latino workers. Title VII of the act was aimed at preventing discrimination on the job. Although initially intended mostly for African Americans, all ethnic groups benefited from the Civil Rights Act.

The United Farm Workers

In the 1960s the plight of migrant farm workers came to the forefront of the American consciousness. Migrant workers move from place to place depending on which fruits and vegetables are in season and need to be picked. These workers suffer through bad living conditions, low wages, and poor schooling for their

Title VII of the 1964 Civil Rights Act
(National Origin Discrimination)

National origin discrimination means treating people unfavorably because they come from another country or because they do not speak English like a native speaker. Title VII of the Civil Rights Act of 1964 prohibits national origin discrimination in employment. In addition to guaranteeing equal wages and fair hiring and firing practices, the law also safeguards against language discrimination. An employer cannot base a workplace decision on an employee's foreign accent unless the accent interferes with job performance.

children. Many of them do not complain because they are in the United States illegally. They are scared of being deported, or sent back, to their home country.

There is no one better known in the cause for migrant workers than César Chávez. Born in 1927, Chávez founded the United Farm Workers union, which led the struggle to gain basic rights for the workers who harvest the nation's agriculture. Under his leadership, farm workers successfully negotiated labor contracts with growers for the first time. After his death in 1993, Chávez received the Presidential Freedom Award posthumously from President Bill Clinton in 1994.

Dolores Huerta co-founded the United Farm Workers union with César Chávez. She helped pave the way for other Latinas in this field. Linda Chavez-Thompson, for example, is a Mexican-American union leader who works to improve conditions for workers. She was the first ethnic minority person ever elected to an executive office of the AFL-CIO, the largest federation of labor unions in the country.

Latinos in the Workforce

Latinos have a higher workforce participation (67%) than Whites, Asians, or African Americans.[5] Yet Latinos continue to have a high poverty rate, with

Dolores Huerta, second in line, marches for workers' rights with the president of the United Farm Workers in 2002.

almost 26% of Hispanic families living in poverty.[6] Part of the reason for this is that Latinos tend to earn less than other workers. When compared to Anglo workers, Latino workers earn about 61 percent of white workers' salaries.[7] Called the "wage gap," this difference in earning power continues to widen. This in turn results in unequal wealth accumulation and decreased opportunities in education, employment, and retirement. But because of their large numbers, Latino purchasing power has been increasing every year. By 2015 Latino purchasing power climbed to $1.5 trillion per year.[8]

Latinos also have the highest work fatality and injury rates in the United States.[9] Latino worker fatalities accounted for 14 percent of the fatal work injuries that occurred in the United States in 2003. This rate is almost 35 percent higher than the rate recorded for all workers. Foreign-born Latino workers have a rate twice that of US-born Latinos. Limited English proficiency, lack of knowledge about safety laws and rights, and fear of retaliation by employers all contribute to this grim situation.

Latinos in the Business World Today

There has been a substantial increase in the number of Latino-owned businesses. In 1977 there were about 219,000 Latino-owned businesses in the United States. Today, there are more than two million.[10] In comparison to other groups, Latino small businesses are growing at twice the rate of the national average. Nearly one-third of Latino-owned businesses are in the construction, repair and maintenance, and personal and laundry services industries.[11] While Latino-owned businesses can be found in all states, they tend to thrive in states with the largest numbers of Latinos (California, Florida, New York, and Texas).

Most Latino-owned businesses are small, family-run enterprises. Grocery stores, bakeries, record shops, and small restaurants that cater primarily to Spanish-speaking clientele can be found in all *barrios* in the United States. Where there are large concentrations of Spanish-speaking immigrants, offices that specialize in translation, immigration services, and check cashing can also be found. But increasingly, Whites and other groups are venturing into Latino neighborhoods, making up an increasingly large share of the businesses' customers.

Latinas are behind much of the growth in small business ownership among Hispanics. In the United States, Latina entrepreneurs start businesses at a rate six times the national average.[12]

Marketing to Latinos

Latinos have a collective buying power of $1.2 trillion.[13] As the percentage of Latinos in the US population increases, businesses recognize that they must consider this group seriously in their marketing efforts. And because Hispanics are on average ten years younger than the general population, this trend will continue in the foreseeable future. Most grocery stores, even those in small communities, stock Latino foods. Almost twice as much salsa is sold in the United States as

Many Latino businesses are small and family-owned, like this food market in North Carolina.

ketchup. Tortillas and taco kits outsell hamburger and hot dog buns now.[14] But Latino influence can be felt beyond common food items. Businesses now realize that Latino preferences in transportation, entertainment, media, and financial services must also be taken into account.

According to the Center for Hispanic Leadership, Latino consumers want products and brands that are relevant to their culture and values.[15] Increasingly, businesses are advertising in both English and Spanish. And because Latinos participate in social media and mobile devices at higher rates than other groups, advertisers are sensitive to reaching this population electronically.[16] As a new report from the Nielsen research company states, "Latinos are a fundamental component to business success."[17]

Latino Buying Power

LATINOS IN THE U.S. ARE...

52.9 MILLION PEOPLE

16.7%
OF THE POPULATION

1 IN EVERY 6 INDIVIDUALS

1 IN EVERY 4 CHILDREN

55%
OF THE POPULATION GROWTH FROM 2000 TO 2011

$1.2 TRILLION IN BUYING POWER

64.6% MEXICAN
9.5% PUERTO RICAN
3.8% SALVADORAN
3.6% CUBAN
2.9% DOMINICAN
2.3% GUATEMALAN
1.9% COLOMBIAN
...AND MORE

LATINO BRANDINGPOWER

SOURCES: U.S. CENSUS BUREAU, AMERICAN COMMUNITY SURVEY, PEW HISPANIC CENTER, SELIG CENTER FOR ECONOMIC GROWTH | VISIT: WWW.LATINOBRANDINGPOWER.COM

The growing numbers of Latinos in the United States means companies are paying attention to their buying power.[18]

Latinos in Management

Although Latinos are the fastest-growing group in the United States, they are also the most underrepresented group in corporate offices and boardrooms. Latinos hold only three percent of the board seats in Fortune 500 corporations. Only one percent of the executive offices at those same companies are occupied by Latinos.[19] Of the twenty female CEOs (chief executive offers) at Fortune 500 companies, only four are women of color and none are Latina.[20] Many frustrated Latino executives point to the "glass ceiling" that Latinos have historically encountered in corporate America. "Glass ceiling" refers to an invisible wall that keeps people from being promoted or advancing in a company. Some industries, such as insurance and telecommunications, have hardly any Latinos at all in executive positions. One notable exception is Verizon's Magda Yrizarry, who has been recognized for her commitment to the Latino community.

Despite the dismal statistics, there have been modest gains in corporate America, as more Latinos are joining the executive ranks. Latinas now make up the fastest growing group of business owners and more are becoming top-level managers.[21] And a recent study of sixty major companies found that nearly all of them have internship programs to recruit Hispanics.[22]

Magda Yrizarry

Magda Yrizarry joined the Verizon corporation in 1990 to direct corporate responsibility and educational initiatives. One of the few Latina executives at a Fortune 500 company, Yrizarry is on LULAC's National Education Service Centers Board and the Corporate Advisory Board of the Hispanic Association on Corporate Responsibility. She is a founding member of 100 Hispanic Women, an organization of Latinas in leadership positions.

Latinos in Contemporary Society

Times were not easy for Sonia Sotomayor when she was growing up in the Bronx neighborhood of New York City in the 1950s and 1960s. Her parents had moved from Puerto Rico to give their family a better life in the United States. But when Sonia was only nine years old, her father, Juan, died. Sonia also developed juvenile diabetes. Her widowed mother, Celina, worked hard to raise Sonia and her sister. Celina emphasized the importance of education and saved up to buy the girls an encyclopedia set to use at home.

While her mother worked long hours, Sonia read Nancy Drew mystery books and loved watching the TV court drama *Perry Mason*. In one episode, the prosecuting attorney was overruled by the judge. At that moment, Sonia realized that the judge had more power than the attorneys and decided that she too would one day be a judge.[1]

After graduating from Cardinal Spellman High School as valedictorian in 1972, Sonia went to

United States Supreme Court Associate Justice Sonia Sotomayor, seen here in 2013, was the first Latina to be named to the US Supreme Court.

Princeton University to study history. Her hard work and good grades had won her a scholarship at the prestigious school. There, she joined a Puerto Rican student organization which she later said provided her "with an anchor I needed to ground myself in that new and different world."[2] She then attended Yale Law School and passed the bar exam in 1980. After working as an attorney in a private practice, she became a US District Court Judge and later appointed to the US Second Circuit Court of Appeals.

In 2009 President Barack Obama named Sotomayor to the Supreme Court. She was the first Latina Supreme Court Justice in US history.

Today Latinos can be found in all aspects of American society—in the law, education, the military, sports, the arts, and entertainment. With approximately 54 million Hispanics making up about 17% of the population, they are the largest ethnic minority in the United States. While once they were barely seen on television or in the media, today the Latino presence is evident in all walks of life.

Latino Literature

Latino literature is especially rich and vibrant. From the time of colonization to the present-day United States, Latinos have been writing about their experiences and developing new forms of creative literature.

Much of Latino literature has had a political bent, describing injustices and struggles in the United States. Luís Valdez, a playwright and actor, is widely credited as the founder of the Chicano theater movement. Born to migrant farm workers, he incorporated much of what he experienced as a child into plays performed by *El Teatro Campesino* (The Peasants Theater). In 1987 Valdez achieved popular acclaim with his screenplay for *La Bamba*.

Mexican-American Sandra Cisneros addresses many issues specific to Latinas through her writing. Her experiences growing up in Chicago's poor South

Sandra Cisneros is an American writer of Mexican descent. Her novel *The House on Mango Street* chronicles a young Latina's childhood in a poor Chicago neighborhood.

El Teatro Campesino
(The Peasants Theater)

Founded in 1965, *El Teatro Campesino* is a theatrical group that reflects the Chicano experience. Founded by Luís Valdéz, El Teatro Campesino was originally started when the United Farm Workers union was on strike for better work conditions. Valdéz wanted to bring entertainment to the workers and encourage the strikers in their hard work.

He approached union leader César Chávez about staging a performance. Valdéz remembers Chávez's reaction: "'There is no money, no actors. Nothing. Just workers on strike.' But he also told me that if I could put something together, it was OK with him. And that was all we needed—a chance. We jumped on top of a truck and started performing. Then something great happened. Our work raised the spirits of everyone on the picket lines and César saw that."[3] Using simple props, masks, and signs, El Teatro Campesino created skits that spoofed the growers and educated people about important issues.

Valdéz also went on to direct films such as *Zoot Suit* and *La Bamba*. His work has been recognized in a number of ways. He is the recipient of the Presidential Medal of the Arts, the Aguila Azteca Award, and the Governor's Award from the California Arts Council.

Luís Valdéz was the founder of El Teatro Campesino.

Side led to her highly praised novel *The House on Mango Street* (1984). In 1995 she received the MacArthur Fellowship "Genius Grant" for her work.

Other Latino authors recount the challenges of immigration. Dominican-American Julia Alvarez published *How the Garcia Girls Lost Their Accents* in 1991. This sensitive story tells of four sisters who must adjust to life in America after fleeing from the Dominican Republic. Told through a series of episodes, the story unfolds in reverse chronology, starting in adulthood and moving backward to their comfortable childhood on the island. Adapting to American life is difficult. It causes embarrassment when friends meet their parents and anger as they are bullied and called "spics." The interconnected stories offer perspectives through Dominican eyes.

Cuban-American Oscar Hijuelos was the first Latino to win the Pulitzer Prize for fiction. His novel *The Mambo Kings Play Songs of Love* (1989) was so popular it was also made into a movie. *The Mambo Kings* tells the story of two Cuban brothers who immigrate to the United States in the 1950s, during the height of the mambo craze. The brothers' dreams of becoming mambo kings do not go exactly as planned, but the bonds of family and culture are evident throughout the story.

Mexican-American author and poet Gary Soto has written dozens of books for children and young adults. Born in California, his family lived in a working-class barrio in Fresno. These childhood memories form the basis of many of his works. He says, "Even though I

Mexican-American author Gary Soto writes poetry and books for young people.

write a lot about life in the barrio, I am really writing about the feelings and experiences of most American kids."[4] His picture books, such as *Too Many Tamales*, give a glimpse into Latino families.

María Irene Fornés is a Cuban-American playwright who has written more than thirty-five plays, many of them about the lives of Latinas. She has won nine Obie Awards, the highest award for off-Broadway plays. In addition to writing, she helps young Latinos get started in the theater by teaching and mentoring.

Pedro Pietri
(1944–2004)

Pietri was born in Ponce, Puerto Rico, and moved with his family to the Harlem neighborhood of New York City in 1947. A member of the Young Lords when the group was active, Pietri composed provocative poetry, plays, and artwork, giving voice to many of the hardships Latinos faced. He died of stomach cancer in 2004.

His best known work is the poem "Puerto Rican Obituary." In this poem published in 1973, Pietri recounts the experiences of many Puerto Ricans who migrate to New York in search of the American dream, only to meet discrimination and suffering.

Pedro Pietri

Puerto Rican author Esmeralda Santiago has received numerous awards for her writing. Her coming-of-age story, *When I Was Puerto Rican*, is both sad and inspirational. Immigrating to the United States when she was thirteen years old, she went on to attend New York City's Performing Arts High School, Sarah Lawrence College, and Harvard University. Today, Santiago works as a community activist on behalf of the arts and young people.

A mural tribute by artist Chico memorializes poet Pedro Pietri on the façade of the Nuyorican Poets Cafe in New York in 2005.

Chilean novelist Isabel Allende gained acclaim in the United States with her book *House of the Spirits.* When the novel was made into a movie ten years later, she gained new fans of her work. In addition to the many lectures and book tours she gives throughout the world, Allende is heavily involved in the Isabel Allende Foundation. The foundation helps children and women in need. Through scholarships and grants, the organization furthers education, provides health care, and promotes peace.

Richard Blanco was the first Latino to be named the US Inaugural Poet. At Barack Obama's second presidential inauguration, Blanco read aloud his poem, "One Today," which he called "a humble, modest poem, one presented to a national audience as a gift of comradeship..."[5] Born in Madrid, Spain, of Cuban descent, Blanco's 2014 book, *Prince of Los Cocuyos*, is a bittersweet memoir of growing up in a Cuban household in Miami, Florida.

The Nuyorican Poets Café

The Nuyorican Poets Café is located in a small building in New York City's Lower East Side. Passersby might be surprised to learn that inside the humble-looking building some of the most creative Latino poets, actors, and musicians share their work.

Inside, people of all ages and colors sit on bar stools, crouch on the floor, or simply lean against the brick walls covered with posters and artwork. As someone takes to the small stage, a hush comes over the room. For the next few hours, well-known authors

Richard Blanco

One Today

One sun rose on us today, kindled
*   over our shores,*
peeking over the Smokies, greeting
*   the faces*
of the Great Lakes, spreading a
*   simple truth*
across the Great Plains, then
*   charging across the Rockies.*
One light, waking up rooftops,
*   under each one, a story*
told by our silent gestures moving
*   behind windows.*

as well as amateurs will read their poetry and spark lively discussion.

Called one of "the living treasures of New York" by the Municipal Society of New York, the café began in 1973 in the living room of professor and poet Miguel Algarín. With the help of Pedro Pietri and Miguel Piñero, within two years the popularity of the poetry "slams" was so great that a nearby building was rented. Eventually a building was bought in 1980 and the Nuyorican Poets Café became a permanent institution. While the café may be best known for its plays and poetry slams, it is also a venue for hip-hop, films, and music.[6] It provides a window into Latino culture and history as expressed through the voices of some of America's most renowned Latino artists.

Latino Scientists

Latinos have contributed much to the fields of medicine and science. Since the founding of the nation, Latinos have taken care of the sick, developed new agricultural methods, and invented new machines to improve human life.

Ynés Mexia was a Mexican-American botanist who conducted pioneering research in the medicinal properties of plants. She made many trips through North and South America in the early 1900s, collecting, classifying, and photographing thousands of plant specimens. Mexia is credited with discovering one new plant genus of *Compositae* and more than five hundred new plant species.

In 1959 Dr. Severo Ochoa won the Nobel Prize in physiology medicine for his work on the synthesis of RNA (ribonucleic acid), one of the chemical building blocks of life. In 1986 Costa Rican-born Dr. Franklin Chang-Díaz, the first Latino astronaut, went into space. In 1993 Dr. Ellen Ochoa became the first Latina in space when she flew on the shuttle *Discovery*. Also an inventor, Ochoa holds three patents in optical processing.

The chief doctor in the United States is called the Surgeon General. In 1990 Antonia Novello was the first Latina—and first woman—to be appointed

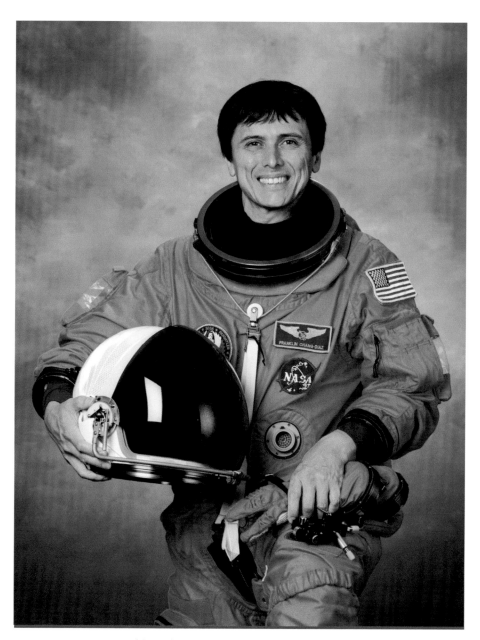

Dr. Franklin Chang-Díaz was the first Latino in space.

as the nation's Surgeon General. As a child in Puerto
Rico, she was frequently hospitalized with an illness
that caused her great discomfort. It was not until
she was twenty years old that she was able to get the
surgery that would fix her condition.[7] As Surgeon
General, Novello worked hard to get better health care
for children. She also called for special attention to the
problems of alcoholism, smoking, AIDS, and violence.

Mexican-American chemist Dr. Mario Molina
won a Nobel Prize in 1995 for his research on how
human-made chemicals affect the ozone. For his
pioneering work, he received the Presidential Medal
of Freedom from President Obama in 2013.

Latinos in the Military

Latinos have fought in every US war, serving their
country well and earning honors and awards. During the
US Civil War, nearly ten thousand Mexican Americans
served in regular or volunteer units. Many Cubans also
fought, serving in both the Union and Confederate
armies. In the Spanish-American War, a large number
of Latinos, primarily Mexican Americans, served
to end the war with Spain. In 1917, just before the
United States entered World War I, Puerto Ricans were
granted US citizenship and became eligible for military service. Subsequently, eighteen thousand Puerto
Ricans served in the war.

During World War II, more than four hundred
thousand Latinos served in the US Armed Forces,
more than any other ethnic group. At least sixty-five
thousand were Puerto Rican, including two hundred

Ellen Ochoa, Astronaut and Engineer

Ellen Ochoa was valedictorian of her class when she graduated from Grossmont High School in La Mesa, California, in 1975, and again five years later when she earned the baccalaureate degree in physics from San Diego University. With a Stanford engineering fellowship and an IBM predoctoral fellowship, Ochoa earned a master of science degree in electrical engineering from Stanford University in 1981, and a PhD, also in electrical engineering, in 1985.

Ellen Ochoa

Ochoa became interested in aviation and applied to the NASA space program. After being rejected at first, Ochoa was finally selected as an astronaut from close to two thousand applicants. In 1990 she became the first Latina selected for the space shuttle program. And when the space shuttle *Discovery* roared into space in April 1993, Ochoa became the first Latina to travel into space.

puertoriqueñas who served in the Women's Army Corps. When these veterans returned from the war, they used their G.I. benefits to further their education and buy homes. Twelve Latinos earned the Medal of Honor during World War II.

Latinos also distinguished themselves in a number of ways in the Korean War. The *Borinqueneers*, the 65th Regimental Combat Team from Puerto Rico, earned their commander's highest praise when he wrote *Puerto Rico's Fighting 65th US Infantry: From San Juan to Chorwau*. General William Harris wrote, "No ethnic group has greater pride in itself and its heritage than the Puerto Rican people. Nor have I encountered any that can be more dedicated and zealous in its support of the democratic principles for which the United States stands. Many Puerto Ricans

US Army soldiers of the 130th Engineer Battalion of the Puerto Rico National Guard conduct training in Salinas, Puerto Rico.

have fought to the death to uphold them."[8] During the Vietnam conflict, eighty thousand Latinos served in the Armed Forces. And during the Persian Gulf War of 1990–1991, close to twenty-five thousand Latino men and women served in the operations Desert Shield and Desert Storm.

Currently, there are more than 157,000 Latinos on active duty, about 11% of the military forces.[9] These numbers are expected to grow as all three branches of the Armed Forces increase their recruitment of Latinos. And at all the US military academies, the percentage of Latino students is on the rise. To date, sixty Hispanic Americans have earned the Congressional Medal of Honor, the nation's highest military award.[10]

Latinos in Sports

Latinos have long contributed to sports in the United States. In 1871 Esteban Bellán was the first Latino to play major league baseball. Since then, Latinos have excelled at the sport. Roberto Clemente, one of baseball's greatest players of all time, won twelve Gold Glove Awards and was the first Puerto Rican to be voted Most Valuable Player. He was a great humanitarian as well. Born in Puerto Rico in 1934, he worked tirelessly to improve the condition of the poor in his homeland. He died in a plane crash in 1972, en route to take badly needed supplies to earthquake victims in Nicaragua. He was elected to the Baseball Hall of Fame in 1973.

Roberto Clemente was a successful professional baseball player who spent much of his off-season doing charity work.

Dominican-American Alex Rodriguez has received many awards for his excellent playing as a shortstop. In that position, he holds the record for most home runs in a single season. He was named the 2003 Most Valuable Player in the American League. Called A-Rod by his many fans, Rodriguez is also known for his charitable giving. In 2002 Mark Light Stadium in Miami, Florida, was renamed Alex Rodriguez Park after he donated $3.9 million to renovate the facility. He also established a Boys and Girls Club and donated two hundred thousand dollars to a children's mental health center in Washington Heights, New York.

Great Latino names in professional golf include Lee Trevino, Chi Chi Rodriguez, and Nancy Lopez. Puerto Rican Chi Chi Rodríguez was inducted into PGA's World Golf Hall of Fame in 1992. Mexican-American Lee Trevino was 1971's PGA Player of Year.

Mexican-American professional golfer Nancy Lopez is widely regarded as one of the greatest women golfers of all time. She began to play golf when she was eight years old and was only twelve years old when she won the New Mexico Women's Amateur tournament. Winning forty-eight titles, she is one of the top pro golf money winners of all time. In 1989 she became the youngest player ever inducted into the LPGA's World Golf Hall of Fame.

There are now many Latinos on the professional tennis circuit. Argentinian-American Gabriela Sabatini was the US Open singles champion in 1990. Dominican-American Mary Joe Fernández was on the

Mexican-American golfer Nancy Lopez won forty-eight
LPGA tour events, including three major championships.

US Olympic Team in 1992 and 1996, and won a gold
medal in 1992.

Historically, professional basketball has not
had many Latino players. However, in recent years
Argentine Emanuel "Manu" Ginóbili, Mexican-born
Eduardo Najera, Dominican-American Francisco
García, and Carlos Arroyo from Puerto Rico have all

played with major teams in the National Basketball Association.

Football is another sport in which Latinos have not been well represented. This is in part because American football is not popular in other parts of the world. Still, there have been some noteworthy Latinos who have played. The first Latino player in the National Football League was Joseph Aguirre who was drafted in 1941 by the Washington Redskins. Mexican-American quarterback Jim Plunkett led the Raiders to two Super Bowl victories. Anthony Muñoz played thirteen seasons for the Cincinnati Bengals, considered one of the best offensive tackles ever. Tony Gonzalez, one of the most celebrated tight ends in NFL history, had a successful seventeen-year career and now is an analyst for *The NFL Today*.

Although soccer is the most popular sport in the world, its popularity has been slow to grow in the United States. Since the 1990s this has changed, in large part due to the growing number of Latinos and immigrants from Latin America who follow and participate in the sport. Major League Soccer reports that 25 percent of its players are Hispanic. On the US National Men's team, standout players have included Michael Orozco, Alejandro Bedoya, Alfredo Morales, Joe Corona, José Torres, Omar González, Hérculez Gómez, and Nick Rimando. Claudio Reyna captained the US World Cup squads in 2002 and 2006, and Carlos Bocanegra was the US captain in the 2010 World Cup. And since 40 percent of Major League Soccer's youth academy participants are Hispanic, the

Carlos Bocanegra

number of Latinos playing *fútbol*, as it is known in Spanish, is sure to increase. "Major League Soccer got it years ago," says Michael Lewis of FOX Sports Latino. "The future is Latino and in many respects, that future is now."[11]

Latinos in Hollywood

Since the beginning of the history of Hollywood films, during the silent film age, Latinos have been entertaining the country. Hispanic actresses like Myrtle González, Dolores del Río, and Beatriz Michelena were popular silent film stars. Many of these film stars made the transition to "talkies" in the 1920s and 1930s. Films in subsequent decades featured actors such as Fernando Lamas, Anthony Quinn, Rita Hayworth, José Ferrer, Ricardo Montalbán, Chita Rivera, and Rita Moreno.

Perhaps the most well-known of all Cuban entertainers was Desi Arnaz. Born to wealthy parents in Santiago de Cuba, Arnaz and his family fled to the United States after a revolution in 1933 left them in peril. By the late 1930s, he was well-known in the United States as a bandleader, musician, and singer. But it was when he married Lucille Ball and costarred with her on *I Love Lucy* that he earned worldwide

Rita Moreno

Rita Moreno is only one of two artists who have won all four major entertainment awards (the Oscar for films, the Emmy for television, the Tony for theater, and the Grammy for music). Born Rosa Dolores Alverio in Humacao, Puerto Rico, she moved to New York City at the age of five. She soon began a career in acting, often singing and dancing as well. She is best known for her performance as Anita in the film *West Side Story* and as a regular cast member on TV's *The Electric Company*. In June 2004, she received the Presidential Medal of Freedom from President George W. Bush for her contributions to American culture.

Rita Moreno

acclaim. As a producer, he pioneered the "three-camera" technique, live studio audiences, and was the first to use film to preserve TV shows for reruns. *I Love Lucy* continues to be one of the most treasured shows of all time.

Puerto Rican actor Raúl Juliá made a name for himself in movies such as *Kiss of the Spider Woman* and *The Addams Family*. Before that, New York audiences appreciated his roles in Shakespearean plays and Broadway musicals. He was also well known for his humanitarian efforts, especially his desire to end hunger.

Today, Latino stars include Sofia Vergara, Eva Longoria, Andy Garcia, Antonio Banderas, Edward James Olmos, Rosario Dawson, Rosie Pérez, Jennifer López, Esai Morales, Zoe Saldana, and John Leguizamo. As more film producers and directors such as Robert Rodriguez (*Spy Kids, El Mariachi, Desperado*) cast more Latinos in leading roles, Hispanics will be even more visible in Hollywood.

Latinos in Music

The 1940s and 1950s saw the emergence of dance crazes from Latin America. Music and dances known as the rumba, mambo, and chachachá overtook the nation during this time. Based on Afro-Cuban percussion and beats, they formed the basis for later Latin music.

Latinos also made an impact on the rock and roll scene. Ritchie Valens, best known for his hit songs "Donna" and "La Bamba," was born Richard

Desi Arnaz and Lucille Ball starred in the successful sitcom *I Love Lucy* from 1951 to 1957.

Valenzuela in Los Angeles in 1941. His song "La Bamba" was a rock and roll version of a traditional Mexican song. Valens's life was later chronicled in the 1987 movie *La Bamba*. The Mexican-American group Los Lobos rerecorded the hit title song for the movie and a whole new generation discovered his music.

Salsa music (in Spanish, salsa refers to a spicy or flavorful sauce) became very popular in the 1960s and 1970s. Through the work of musicians such as Tito Puente, Willie Colón, Johnny Pacheco, Ray Burretto, Eddie Palmieri, Héctor Lavoe, Celia Cruz, and Rubén Blades, American audiences began to appreciate the multiple sounds and beats this genre could include. Simultaneously, the Latin sounds of Carlos Santana and his band also helped to popularize Latino music.

Merengüe is another type of popular Latino music. Lively and joyful, it is music that is usually danced to. While its origins are disputed, merengüe can be traced to the second half of the eighteenth century. Merengüe, as a music and dance form, is most strongly identified with the Dominican Republic.

In the pop music world, Cuban-American Gloria Estefan brought Latin rhythms to Top 20 songs. As both a singer and musician, Estefan became a beloved performer with hits such as "Conga," "Dr. Beat," and "Rhythm is Gonna Get You."

Reggaeton is also enjoying popularity in the United States. Originating in Panama with reggae beats, reggaeton is a form of dance music very popular with Latino youth. The music is a blend of Jamaican reggae with traditional Latin-American beats and rhythms. It

Salsa dancing continues to be popular with a wide variety of audiences.

Rubén Blades

After moving from Panama to the United States and becoming aware of social issues and injustices in the world, Rubén Blades began to develop his own singing style and wrote salsa songs with a message. Blades is widely credited as being the first salsa singer to write his own songs, and the first to include politics in his music. He was instrumental in developing one of the varieties of salsa known as *salsa conciente.*

One music reviewer feels that the main message in Blades's songs is "to stimulate thought, to raise consciousness." Another journalist wrote that the singer's songs "are not of partying, but of protest."[12]

Blades started a new political party in his homeland and ran for the presidency of Panama. Although he did not win, several party representatives were elected to government positions.

Rubén Blades wrote salsa songs with a message.

is often sung in Spanglish, a mixture of Spanish and English.

Latinos continue to influence American pop music. Christina Aguilera, Selena Gomez, Shakira, and Pitbull have all had top hits on Billboard's Top 10. But most Latino stars are not content to simply have commercial success. Many of them give back to the Latino community. Shakira's "Pies Descalzos" (Bare Feet) Foundation provides education and food for poor children in her native Colombia. Selena Gomez kicked off the UR Votes Count in 2008 to involve more teens in the election process.

Selena Gomez

Latinos in US Popular Culture

American popular culture is heavily influenced by Latino cultures. Many popular "American" foods have their origins in Latino culture. Foods such as tortillas, nachos, and flan have become commonplace in the United States. Pop and hip-hop music often have Latin rhythms or even Spanish words in the lyrics.

Today, the influence of Spanish can be seen in a number of ways in American English. Many cities in the Southwest such as Los Angeles, Santa Fe, and San Diego are testaments to their Hispanic origins. Common "American" words such as *rodeo, mosquito, cargo*, and *patio* all have their origins in the Spanish language.

Spanish-language newspapers and radio and television stations are the norm in many US cities. Daily newspapers such as *Noticias del Mundo* in Los Angeles, *El Nuevo Herald* in Miami, and *El Diario* in New York all serve to keep their readers informed about current events and reinforce their cultures.

In addition to dozens of local Spanish-language stations, Latinos also enjoy several television stations that broadcast nationally. Telemundo and Univision are two companies that offer Spanish-speaking TV programming that includes sports, news, variety shows, and soap operas. More and more channels, such as CNN, Discovery, and National Geographic now offer an *en español* version of their programming as well.

Latinos in Government

Since 1960 more Latinos have been elected to Congress than in the previous 140 years.[13] Still, only 7 percent of the members of Congress are Latino.[14] Most of these government leaders are members of the Congressional Hispanic Caucus, an influential group of lawmakers.

Since it was first established in 1976, the Congressional Hispanic Caucus (CHC) has been trying to improve conditions for Latinos in the United States. It was organized by five Latino Congress members who recognized the special needs of Latinos. The CHC promotes issues such as better health care, bilingual education, and workers' rights.

Spanish language newspapers are widely available throughout the United States.

One member of the CHC, Rubén Hinojosa, is a Representative from Texas. As the son of poor Mexican immigrants, he learned from his parents early on that education was the way to a better life. As the head of the Subcommittee on Higher Education, he works hard to improve Latinos' access to a college education. He points out that while more Latinos are graduating from high school and going to college, there is still much work to be done. Hinojosa believes that many low-income students are qualified to go to college but cannot due to financial barriers. As a result, he argues, many talented people are not developing their full ability.[15]

The CHC was instrumental in getting approval to establish a work group to explore the possibility of creating a National Museum of the American Latino. As part of the Smithsonian Museum complex, this effort would document Latino history, life, and culture. Fundraising is underway with support by Latino Senators Bob Menendez and Marco Rubio and Representatives Xavier Becerra and Ileana Ros-Lehtinen.

Latinos are an important part of the social fabric of the United States. They have played a vital role in many ways. While their history and contributions to the United States are undeniable, Latinos continue to work hard to be a part of American society. Although gains have been made in education, employment, and civil rights, Latinos still face prejudice and discrimination. The new generation of Latinos are picking up where previous generations have left off.

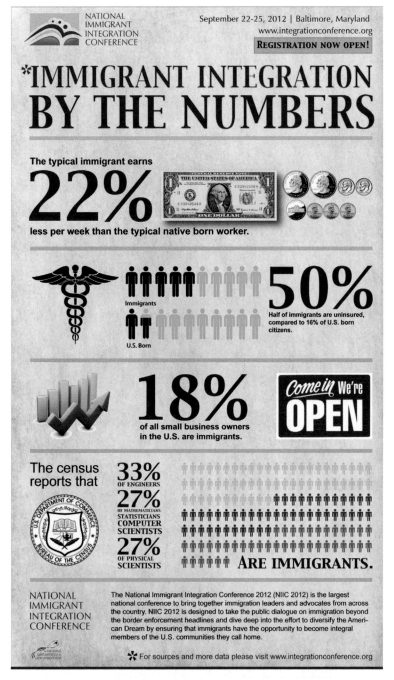

A poster by the National Immigrant Integration Conference gives a snapshot of the immigrant presence in the United States in 2012.[16]

TIMELINE

1492 Columbus embarks on his historic exploratory trip for Spain.

1513 Juan Ponce de León explores *La Florida*.

1565 St. Augustine, the oldest city in the United States, is established by the Spanish in Florida.

1769 Father Junípero Serra establishes a mission in San Diego, California.

1848 The Mexican-American War is brought to an end with the Treaty of Guadalupe Hidalgo.

1898 Puerto Rico and Cuba are ceded by Spain through its defeat in the Spanish-American War.

1910 Seeking safety from the Mexican Revolution, thousands of Mexicans immigrate to the southwest United States.

1917 The Jones Act is passed, granting all Puerto Ricans US citizenship.

1924 Immigration is curtailed and the Border Patrol is founded through an act of Congress.

1942 The Bracero Program is introduced.

1943 The Zoot Suit Riots occur.

1947 Operation Bootstrap begins in Puerto Rico.

1954 Operation Wetback is launched to halt illegal immigration.

1959 Fidel Castro leads a revolution in Cuba, causing thousands to flee to the United States.

1962 César Chávez and his associates found the National Farm Workers Association.

1964 The Civil Rights Act is passed.

1966 César Chávez leads a 340-mile march to bring attention to the plight of the farm workers. Soon after, the United Farm Workers union is formed.

1970 La Raza Unida Party is founded.

1973 The Nuyorican Poets Café is founded in New York City.

1976 The Congressional Hispanic Caucus is established.

1978 Affirmative action is challenged in the case of the *California Regents* v. *Allan Bakke*.

1980 The Mariel boatlift brings 125,000 Cuban refugees to the United States.

1990 Dr. Antonia Novello is the first Latina—and first woman—to be appointed as the nation's Surgeon General.

2006 President George W. Bush assigns an additional 6,000 Border Patrol officers to the US–Mexico border.

2009 Sonia Sotomayor becomes the first Latina Supreme Court Justice in US history.

2011 Latinos become the largest ethnic minority in the United States.

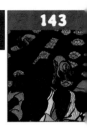

CHAPTER NOTES

Chapter 1. The Struggle for Rights

1. "Education of the Heart–Quotes by Cesar Chavez," *United Farm Workers*, accessed February 25, 2015, http://www.ufw. org/_page.php?menu=research&inc=history/09.html.

2. Susan Ferriss and Ricardo Sandoval, *The Fight in the Fields* (New York: Harcourt Brace, 1997), 119.

3. Jacques E. Levy, *Cesar Chavez: Autobiography of La Causa* (New York: Norton, 1975), 246.

Chapter 2. Latino Americans

1. Miriam Jiménez Román and Juan Flores, *The Afro-Latin@ Reader: History and Culture in the United States*, (Durham, N.C.: Duke University Press, 2010).

2. "Rodolfo Gonzales, Advocate for 'Chicano Power,' 76," *The Boston Globe*, April 15, 2005, http://www.boston. com/news/globe/obituaries/articles/2005/04/15/rodolfo_ gonzales_advocate_for_chicano_power_76.

3. Sharon R. Ennis, Merarys Ríos-Vargas, and Nora G. Albert, "The Hispanic Population: 2010," *US Census Bureau*, May 2011, http://www.census.gov/prod/cen2010/briefs/ c2010br-04.pdf.

4. "Hispanic Trends," Pew Research Center, accessed February 22, 2015, http://www.pewhispanic.org.

5. US Census Bureau, "2013 Population Estimates," *American Fact Finder*, accessed February 22, 2015, http://factfinder2. census.gov/faces/tableservices/jsf/pages/productview.xhtm- l?pid=PEP_2013_PEPASR6H&prodType=table.

6. Ennis, Ríos-Vargas, and Albert, "The Hispanic Population: 2010."

7. Ibid.

8. Ibid.

9. "Hispanic Population Facts: A Look at Latinos by the Numbers," *The Huffington Post*, September 18, 2013, US Census Bureau: 2012 Population Estimates, http://www.huffingtonpost.com/2013/09/18/hispanic-population-facts_n_3950673.html.
10. Anna Brown and Mark Hugo Lopez, "Mapping the Latino Population, By State, County and City," *Pew Research Center*, August 29, 2013, http://www.pewhispanic.org/2013/08/29/mapping-the-latino-population-by-state-county-and-city/.
11. The Trans-Atlantic Slave Trade Database, *Voyages*, (2009), http://www.slavevoyages.org/tast/index.faces.

Chapter 3. History of Latinos in the United States

1. Mel Martinez, "Secretary Martinez's Remarks at the Hispanic Heritage Month Closing Ceremony," *US Department of Housing and Urban Development*, September 12, 2001, http://archives.hud.gov/remarks/martinez/hispanic heritage.cfm.
2. James A. Lewis, "Las Damas de la Havana, el Precursor, and Francisco de Saavedra," *The Americas* 37, no. 1 (July 1980): 83–99.
3. "The Félix Longoria Affair," *Hispanic Online*, accessed June 15, 2006, http://www.hispaniconline.com/hh02/history_heritage_sidebar_felix_longoria.html.
4. "Pedro Pan," *All Things Considered,* National Public Radio, May 3, 2000, http://www.npr.org/templates/story/story.php?storyId=1073679.
5. Yvonne Conde, *Operation Pedro Pan: The Untold Exodus of 14,048 Cuban Children* (New York: Routledge, 1999), xiii.

Chapter 4. Legal and Civil Rights

1. George Ochoa, *The New York Public Library Amazing Hispanic American History* (New York: John Wiley and Sons, 1998), 71.

2. Rodolfo Acuña, *Occupied America* (New York: Longman, 2000), 272.

3. Dolores Huerta, "Reflection on the UFW Experience," July/August, *Center Magazine*, vol. 18, 1985, 2.

4. "Rodolfo Gonzales, Advocate for 'Chicano Power,' 76," *The Boston Globe online*, April 15, 2006, http://www.boston.com/news/globe/obituaries/articles/2005/04/15/rodolfo_gonzales_advocate_for_chicano_power_76.

5. "Young Lords Party 13-Point Program and Platform," *The Sixties Project*, accessed May 4, 2006, http://lists.village.virginia.edu/sixties/HTML_docs/Resources/Primary/Manifestos/Young_Lords_platform.html.

6. "Civil Rights Act (1964)," *Our Documents.gov*, accessed February 17, 2015, http://www.ourdocuments.gov/doc.php?doc=97.

7. Naleo Educational Fund, *National Directory of Latino Elected Officials*, 5, accessed February 18, 2015, http://www.naleo.org/downloads/2014_National_Directory_of_Latino_Elected_Officials.pdf.

8. Susan Page, "Bush is Opening Doors with a Diverse Cabinet," *USA Today*, December 9, 2004, http://www.usatoday.com/news/washington/2004-12-09-diverse-us-at_x.htm.

9. Vanessa Cardenas and Sophia Kerby, "The State of Latinos in the United States," *Center for American Progress*, August 8, 2012, https://www.americanprogress.org/issues/race/report/2012/08/08/11984/the-state-of-latinos-in-the-united-states/.

10. Mark Hugo Lopez, "The Hispanic Vote in the 2008 Election," *Pew Research Center*, November 5, 2008, http://www.pewhispanic.org/2008/11/05/the-hispanic-vote-in-the-2008-election/.

11. Mark Hugo Lopez and Paul Taylor, "Hispanic Trends," *Pew Research Center*, November 7, 2012, http://www.pewhispanic.org/2012/11/07/latino-voters-in-the-2012-election.

12. *NCLR Voter Guide* (Washington, D.C.: NCLR, 2006).

13. Paul Taylor, Ana Gonzalez-Barrera, Jeffrey S. Passel, and Mark Hugo Lopez, "An Awakened Giant: The Hispanic

Electorate is Likely to Double by 2030," *Pew Research Center,* November 14, 2012, http://www.pewhispanic.org/2012/11/14/an-awakened-giant-the-hispanic-electorate-is-likely-to-double-by-2030/.
14. *NCLR Voter Guide,* 1.

Chapter 5. Latinos and Schooling
1. Robert F. Kennedy, "University of Georgia Law School 1961," *Robert F. Kennedy Center for Justice & Human Rights,* May 6, 1961, http://rfkcenter.org/university-of-georgia-law-school-1961?lang=en.
2. Rebecca Contreras, "East Los Angeles Students Walkout for Educational Reform," *Global Nonviolent Action Database,* (Swarthmore, PA: Swarthmore College, 2011), http://nvdatabase.swarthmore.edu/content/east-los-angeles-students-walkout-educational-reform-east-la-blowouts-1968.
3. Carter Smith and David Lindroth, *Hispanic-American Experience on File.* (New York: Facts on File, Inc., 1999), 6.18.
4. US Census Bureau, "Table 229. Educational Attainment by Race and Hispanic Origin: 1970 to 2010," US Statistical Abtract of the United States, 2012, http://www.census.gov/compendia/statab/2012/tables/12s0229.pdf, and Deborah A. Santiago , Emily Calderón Galdeano, and Morgan Taylor, *The Condition of Latinos in Education: 2015 Factbook* (Washington, D.C.: Excelencia in Education), http://www.edexcelencia.org/research/2015-factbook.
5. Digest of Education Statistics, "Percentage of High School Dropouts among Persons 16 through 24 Years Old (Status Dropout Rate), by Sex and Race/Ethnicity: Selected Years, 1960 through 2012," National Center for Education Statistics, accessed February 18, 2015, http://nces.ed.gov/programs/digest/d13/tables/dt13_219.70.asp.
6. Amanda Paulson, "Dropout Rates High but Fixes Under Way," *Christian Science Monitor,* March 3, 2006, 1.
7. Frederick P. Aguirre, "*Méndez* v. *Westminster School District*: How It Affected *Brown* v. *Board of Education,*" *Journal of Hispanic Higher Education* 4, no. 4 (October 2005): 321–332.

8. Ibid., 322.

9. *Lau* v. *Nichols*, 414 U.S. 563, CERTIORARI TO THE UNITED STATES COURT OF APPEALS FOR THE NINTH CIRCUIT, No. 72-6520, argued December 10, 1973, decided January 21, 1974, accessed June 29, 2006, http://www.law.cornell.edu/supct/html/historics/USSC_CR_0414_0563_ZS.html.

10. "English Language in Public Schools Initiative Statute," accessed February 23, 2015, http://primary98.sos.ca.gov/VoterGuide/Propositions/227text.htm.

11. Rojas, Mary Alexandra, "An examination of U.S. Latino Identities as Constructed in/through Curricular Materials," *Linguistics and Education* 24, no. 3 (September 2013): 373–380.

12. "Affirmative Action Critical to Latino Advancement," *LULAC.org*, accessed February 17, 2015, http://www.lulac.net/advocacy/press/2003/affirmaction.html.

13. "Missouri English Official Language, Amendment 1 (2008)," *Ballotpedia*, accessed February 23, 2015, http://ballotpedia.org/Missouri_English_Official_Language,_Amendment_1_%282008%29, and "Arizona English as the Official Language, Proposition 103 (2006), *Ballotpedia*, accessed February 23, 2015, http://ballotpedia.org/Arizona_English_as_the_Official_Language,_Proposition_103_%282006%29.

14. Roque Planas, "California Bill Would Require High Schools To Offer Ethnic Studies," *Huffington Post*, January 15, 2015, http://www.huffingtonpost.com/2015/01/15/california-ethnic-studies_n_6480170.html.

15. "Race to the Top Fund," *US Department of Education*, accessed February 18, 2015, http://www2.ed.gov/programs/racetothetop/index.html.

16. "President's New High School Initiative, Other Proposed Programs Tackle Issues Important to Hispanics," *US Department of Education*, February 23, 2005, http://www.ed.gov/news/pressreleases/2005/02/02232005a.html.

17. "Trends in Higher Education: Published Charges, 2014–2015," *College Board*, accessed February 18, 2015, http://trends.collegeboard.org/college-pricing/figures-tables/published-prices-national.

18. Chris Reinolds, "Bilingual Summer Camp for Gifted Pupils," *The Atlanta Journal-Constitution*, August 10, 2006, 14JF.

19. College Board, *Resources for Increasing Latino Participation and Success in Higher Education* (New York: The College Board, 2008).

Chapter 6. Latino Immigration

1. "SF DACA Success Story – November 2014," *San Francisco Office of Civic Engagement and Immigrant Affairs*, accessed February 19, 2015, https://dacasf.wordpress.com/sf-daca-success.

2. George Ochoa, *The New York Public Library Amazing Hispanic American History* (New York: John Wiley and Sons, 1998), 69.

3. Miriam Jordan, "Undocumented Immigrant Population Levels Off in U.S.," *Wall Street Journal*, November 18, 2014, http://www.wsj.com/articles/undocumented-immigrant-population-levels-off-in-u-s-led-by-mexican-decline-1416330120.

4. Mark Hugo Lopez and Daniel Dockterman, "U.S. Hispanic Country of Origin Counts for Nation, Top 30 Metropolitan Areas," *Pew Research Center*, May 26, 2011, http://www.pewhispanic.org/2011/05/26/us-hispanic-country-of-origin-counts-for-nation-top-30-metropolitan-areas.

5. *Murillo et al.* v. *Musegades*, 809 F. Supp. 487 (W.D. Texas 1992), LexisNexis Academic Index, August 17, 2006.

6. PBS, "The Border: Operation Wetback," accessed February 18, 2015, http://www.pbs.org/kpbs/theborder/history.

7. Amanda Lee Myers, "Lawmakers Say Prosecutor Misinterpreting Immigration Law," *The Associated Press*, LexisNexis, March 4, 2006.

8. "Judge Says Rejecting 15 Cubans Was Wrong," *St. Pete Times*, March 1, 2006, 5B.

9. "Spanish 'Star Spangled Banner'—Touting the American Dream or Offensive Rewrite?" *ABC News*, April 27, 2006, http://www.abcnews.go.com/WNT/story?id=1898460.

10. "The Anthem Ought to Be Sung in English," *St Petersburg Times*, April 29, 2006, 12A.

11. "Spanish 'Star Spangled Banner'—Touting the American Dream or Offensive Rewrite?"

12. Anita Kumar, "Bush Sending Guard to Border," *St. Pete Times*, May 16, 2006, 1A, 4A.

13. "Immigration in America," *National Public Radio*, October 6, 2004, http://www.npr.org/news/specials/polls/2004/immigration.

Chapter 7. Latino Workers

1. "UFCW Celebrates the Life of Dolores Huerta," *United Food and Commercial Workers (UFCW)*, March 2013, http://www.ufcw.org/2014/03/page/4/.

2. "The Archaeology of the 1913–1914 Colorado Coal Field War Project," Colorado Coal Field War Project, *University of Denver*, accessed February 19, 2015, http://www.du.edu/anthro/ludlow.html.

3. "The Bracero Program," *The Farm Workers Web Site*, accessed February 19, 2015, http://www.farmworkers.org/bracerop.html.

4. "Union Members Summary 2005," *US Department of Labor*, accessed June 20, 2006, http://www.bls.gov/news.release/union2.nr0.htm.

5. "Labor Force Characteristics by Race and Ethnicity, 2011," *US Department of Labor and US Bureau of Labor Statistics*, 2012, http://www.bls.gov/cps/cpsrace2011.pdf.

6. Carmen DeNavas-Walt, Bernadette D. Proctor, and Jessica C. Smith. (2013). *Income, Poverty, and Health Insurance Coverage in the United States: 2012* (Washington, DC: US Census Bureau, 2013), http://www.census.gov/prod/2013pubs/p60-245.pdf.

7. US Census Bureau, "Table 699. Median Income of Families by Type of Family in Current and Constant (2009) Dollars: 1990 to 2009," Statistical Abstract of the United States: 2012, http://www.census.gov/compendia/statab/2012/tables/12s0701.pdf.

8. Glenn Llopis, "Advertisers Must Pay Attention to Hispanic Consumers as Rising Trendsetters in 2013," Forbes. January 9, 2013, http://www.forbes.com/sites/glennllopis/2013/01/09/advertisers-must-pay-attention-to-hispanic-consumers-as-rising-trendsetters-in-2013/.

9. Christen G Byler, "Hispanic/Latino Fatal Occupational Injury Rates," Monthly Labor Review (February 2013), http://www.bls.gov/opub/mlr/2013/02/art2full.pdf.

10. US Census Bureau, "Census Bureau Reports Hispanic-Owned Businesses Increase at More Than Double the National Rate," September 21, 2010, https://www.census.gov/newsroom/releases/archives/business_ownership/cb10-145.html.

11. Ibid.

12. Vanessa Cárdenas and Sophia Kerby, "The State of Latinos in the U.S.," Center for American Progress, August 8, 2012, https://www.americanprogress.org/issues/race/report/2012/08/08/11984/the-state-of-latinos-in-the-united-states/.

13. "Latinas Are a Driving Force Behind Hispanic Purchasing Power in the U.S.," August 1, 2013, Nielsen, http://www.nielsen.com/us/en/insights/news/2013/latinas-are-a-driving-force-behind-hispanic-purchasing-power-in-.html.

14. Hispanic Foods and Beverages in the U.S., 5th Ed., PRNewswire, December 31, 2012, http://www.prnewswire.com/news-releases/hispanic-foods-and-beverages-in-the-us-5th-edition-185273172.html.

15. Llopis.

16. 2012 Hispanic Mobile Consumer Trends Study, June 2012, http://centerforhispanicleadership.typepad.com/files/Hispanic_Mobile_Consumer_Trends.pdf.

17. "State of the Hispanic Consumer: The Hispanic Market Imperative," *Nielsen*, April 17, 2002, http://www.nielsen. com/us/en/insights/reports/2012/state-of-the-hispanic-consumer-the-hispanic-market-imperative.html.

18. *Latino Branding Power*, accessed February 19, 2015, http:// latinobrandingpower.com.

19. Julie Bennett, "Boosting the Hispanic Ranks of Corporate America," *CareerJournal.com*, accessed February 28, 2007, http://www.careerjournal.com/myc/diversity/20030321-bennett.html.

20. Kamren Curiel, "50 Latinas Who Rock Fortune 500 Companies," *Latina*, June 10, 2013, http://www.latina.com/lifestyle/ latinas-fortune-500-companies-corporate-america.

21. Sonia G. Benson, ed., *The Hispanic American Almanac*, (New York: Gale, 2003), 343–344.

22. Beth Senka, "Hispanic Heritage Update: Where are the Latina Leaders in Corporate America?" *The Glass Hammer*, October 1, 2014, http://www.theglasshammer.com/news/ 2014/10/01/hispanic-heritage-update-where-are-the-latina-leaders-in-corporate-america/.

Chapter 8. Latinos in Contemporary Society

1. Sheryl Gay Stolberg, "Sotomayor, a Trailblazer and a Dreamer," *The New York Times*, May 26, 2009, http://www. nytimes.com/2009/05/27us/politics/27websotomayor. html?pagewanted=all&_r=0.

2. "Sonia Sotomayor," *Biography.com*, 2015, http://www. biography.com/people/sonia-sotomayor-453906.

3. Max Benavidez, "Cesar Chavez Nurtured Seeds of Art," *Los Angeles Times*, April 28, 1993, 1.

4. "Gary Soto Biography," *Encyclopedia of World Biography*, accessed February 19, 2015, http://www.notablebiographies. com/news/Sh-Z/Soto-Gary.html.

5. Tucker, Ken, "Poetry at the Presidential Inauguration: The Richard Blanco Poem 'One Today,' Its Form and Meaning," *Entertainment Weekly*, January 21, 2013, http://www.ew.com/ article/2013/01/21/inaugural-richard-blanco.

6. *Nuyorican Poet's Café*, accessed June 22, 2006, http://www.nuyorican.org.

7. "Antonia Novello, M.D.," *Academy of Achievement*, accessed February 19, 2015, http://www.achievement.org/autodoc/page/nov0bio-1.

8. "On the Battlefront," *Hispanic Online*, accessed June 15, 2006, http://www.hispaniconline.com/hh02/history_heritage_on_the_battlefront.html.

9. Erika L Sánchez, "U.S. Military, a Growing Latino Army," *NBC Latino*, January 1, 2013, http://nbclatino.com/2013/01/01/u-s-military-a-growing-latino-army/.

10. "Hispanic Medal of Honor Recipients," *Hispanic Medal of Honor Society*, accessed February 19, 2015, http://www.hispanicmedalofhonor.com/recipients.html.

11. Michael Lewis, "The Rise of Latinos in Major League Soccer," *Fox News Latino*, March 12, 2012, http://latino.foxnews.com/latino/sports/2012/03/12/rise-latinos-in-major-league-soccer.

12. Anthony DePalma, "Ruben Blades: Up From Salsa," *New York Times Biographical Service 18*, no. 6, June 1987, 595.

13. "Hispanic Americans in Congress, 1822–1995," *The Library of Congress*, accessed February 28, 2007, http://www.loc.gov/rr/hispanic/congress/introduction.html.

14. Jennifer Manning, "Membership of the 113th Congress: A Profile," *Congressional Research Service*, November 24, 2014, http://www.senate.gov/CRSReports/crs-publish.cfm?pid=%260BL%2BR\C%3F%0A.

15. Doug Lederman, "The House's New Face on Higher Ed," *Inside Higher Ed*, February 16, 2007, http://www.inside-highered.com/news/2007/02/16/hinojosa.

16. Florida State Hispanic Chamber of Commerce, http://www.fshcc.com/florida-immigration-reform-articles/bid/86610/INFOGRAPHIC-Immigration-Integration-by-the-Numbers.

GLOSSARY

barrio—Neighborhood or section of a city in which Latinos live.

boycott—Not buying a particular product as a means of protest.

bracero—Manual laborer.

Chicano/Chicana—A person of Mexican descent originating from the Spanish word "Mexicano." While it was at first considered an insult, by the 1960s, Mexican-American activists began using the term with pride.

class action suit—A lawsuit by one or more people on behalf of a large group of people with the same interest or issue.

coyotes—People who help smuggle immigrants into the United States.

defect—To leave a country and adopt a new one.

deport—To force a person to leave a country.

diaspora—The scattering of people far from their homeland.

Hispanic—Someone whose family comes from Spanish-speaking countries in Latin America; considered by some, who prefer the term "Latino," to have too much stress on European roots.

Latino/Latina—Someone whose family comes from Spanish-speaking countries in Latin America; often used interchangeably with "Hispanic" although some favor "Latino" because it puts more emphasis on Latin-American origins.

Latin@—A term that includes Latinas and Latinos (females and males) as a whole group.

La Raza—Spanish for "the race." The term was popularly used in the 1960s by Mexican-American political activists. Today the term is used by other Hispanic Americans as well.

maquiladora—Factory along the United States–Mexico border where goods are produced under a program that allows owners to pay little or no taxes.

marielitos—Cubans who emigrated to the United States on the Mariel Boatlift in 1980.

mestizaje—A mixed heritage of European, native, African, and Asian peoples.

mutualistas—Mutual aid societies.

refugee—A person fleeing persecution in his or her homeland.

strike—The stopping of work by employees to demand better conditions and/or higher wages.

wetback—A derogatory term for those immigrants, usually Mexican, who cross the Río Grande into the United States.

FURTHER READING

Books

Brimner, Larry Dane. *Strike! The Farm Workers' Fight for Their Rights.* Honesdale, Penn.: Calkins Creek Publishing, 2014.

Carlisle, Rodney P., ed. *The Hispanic Americans.* New York: Facts on File, 2011.

Carreira, María M. and Beeman, Tom. *Voces: Latino Students on Life in the United States.* Santa Barbara, Calif.: Praeger, 2014.

Kleyn, Tatyana. Immigration: *The Ultimate Teen Guide.* Lanham, Md.: Scarecrow Press, 2011.

Kootz, Russell. *Understanding Your Civil Rights.* New York: Rosen, 2012.

Web Sites

pbs.org/wgbh/latinmusicusa
> *Learn about the history of Latin music, listen to the songs, and see famous Latin musicians perform.*

video.pbs.org/program/latino-americans
> *Latino Americans is a documentary series that explores the history and experiences of Latinos in America.*

teacher.scholastic.com/activities/hispanic/history.htm
> *Read biographies of important Latinos in American history.*

timeforkids.com/minisite/hispanic-heritage-month-1
> *Learn more about Americans of Hispanic heritage through articles, videos, photos, interviews, and biographies.*

INDEX